HAUNTED ATCHISON

T0274654

BROOKE MONTOYA

Haunted America

Published by Haunted America
A Division of The History Press
Charleston, SC
www.historypress.com

First published 2024

Manufactured in the United States

ISBN 9781467155656

Library of Congress Control Number: 2023948364

Notice: The information in this book is true and complete to the best of our knowledge. It is offered without guarantee on the part of the author or The History Press. The author and The History Press disclaim all liability in connection with the use of this book.

HAUNTED
ATCHISON

To my three boys: Bryce, Dylan and Myles,
who are the true loves of my life and my biggest hype men.

CONTENTS

CONTENTS

FOREWORD

T he most haunted city in Kansas."
It's a bold claim. Generally speaking, in my capacity as a paranormal investigator and author, I shy away from "most haunted" statements. They're usually subjective and impossible to prove or disprove. But when it comes to Atchison, it's hard to deny that a strong case can be made.

The city was named after what some claim to have been the shortest-termed president of the United States, David Rice Atchison. It is said that he served in the presidency for just a single day, in a twenty-four-hour gap between the terms of outgoing president James Polk and incoming president Zachary Taylor. It's a claim that has been refuted but continues to make the rounds, perhaps based on the premise of not letting the facts get in the way of a good story.

The same principle holds true when it comes to investigating the ghosts of Atchison. Accounts of hauntings abound from locations across the city, spanning multiple decades and centuries. Brooke Montoya, the author of the book you are now reading, has certainly had her work cut out for her in separating legend and lore from the unvarnished facts. Sometimes, this proves to be all but impossible, though she has left no stone unturned in making the attempt.

During my last visit to Atchison, conducting research for my upcoming book about the Sallie House, I dropped in to visit the city's chamber of commerce in order to pick up a souvenir or two. While paying for my merchandise (Sallie House refrigerator magnets and T-shirts, anyone?), I was asked in a friendly way about the purpose for my visit. When I told the lady behind the counter, she laughed and said that Sallie—said by some to be the ghost of a little girl who died in the house—brought more visitors to Atchison than the city's most famous heroine, the pioneering aviator Amelia Earhart.

I can well believe it.

Yet there is so much more to Atchison than one small house. Farms and railroad depots; theaters and mansions; breweries and cemeteries; all of these places and many more have their ghost stories. So, turn the page and allow Brooke Montoya to guide you on a tour of Atchison's night side, which you will never forget.

—Richard Estep
Longmont, Colorado

ACKNOWLEDGEMENTS

T hank you first and foremost to my family: Bryce, Dylan and Myles. Bryce, you were the first one with me to Atchison, Kansas, when we toured the McInteer Villa. Myles, thank you for being my research assistant. Dylan, thank you for always watching your sibling dogs while I was away researching.

Thank you to my paranormal investigation team, Afterlife Paranormal Investigations of Oklahoma (API of Oklahoma), Tammy Christine and Jill Stokes. You all started as teammates and became two of my closest friends. The adventures over the last four years with you both have been some of the best times of my life. Thank you for always rooting me on, going into all the dark basements and helping me collect research and evidence. Tammy, thank you for the adventures during my research. Jill, thank you for listening to all the stories as I wrote them. You two are the best!

Thank you, January Foster, my best girl, for being my emotional support person through all the ups and downs of this adventure. Thank you for being my number-one fan and always reminding me to believe in myself because you believe in me.

Thank you, Stephanie O'Reilly, for all the McInteer Villa stays when I came up and for making us always feel welcome. Your house was the inspiration for this book. Because of our Villa adventures and coming to Atchison so many times to be at the house, I fell in love with the stories of this town.

Thank you to Steve Caplinger, Sterling Falk and other employees at the Atchison Historical Society for hours of locating pictures, sharing information, answering my questions, finding me space to research and always having smiles on your faces to greet me.

Thank you to Bill RavenHearse, for sharing your home and its history with the two strange ladies who knocked on your door. Thank you to George Pruett, for welcoming us three stalkers to tour the Blish home and sharing its lovely history with us. Thank you, Les, for the extra haunted tales and your gracious welcome. Thank you, Steve Trumble and Mike Burke with UHaunted, for the haunted tour of the town and sharing with me the Maple House and its stories. Thank you, Anne Pruett, Revekka Tsamolias and Margie Begley, for the amazing food, sharing stories and letting me explore your restaurants. Thank you, Sharon Berry, for the book you shared about Hannah and our wonderful conversations about your home. Thank you, Rob Adams, for allowing us into the Dilgert home to investigate and for the copy of Keli Adams's book. Thank you, Lauren, for sitting with us during the investigation and giving us feedback on what we discovered. Thank you, Travis Grossman, for your time and the tour of Theatre Atchison. You are so knowledgeable about the town and have such passion for the city and theater! Thank you, Heather Roesh, for letting us in the Amelia Earhart Birthplace Museum after hours to answer my questions and allow me to investigate. Thank you, Marsha Adair, for trusting me and sharing your thoughts of your beautiful home. Thank you to Evah Cray Museum, for the materials I needed. Thanks also goes to the City of Atchison and Visit Atchison, for answering questions and being so kind and helpful in every way possible.

Thank you to Greg Bakun, who took the cover photo of the McInteer Villa, and to others who contributed pictures for the book. Thank you to all the other welcoming Atchison citizens we met, talked to and reached out via social media to share stories with me. Everyone has been so friendly and accommodating.

Thank you, Tanya McCoy and Jeff Provine, for answering all of my "newbie" author questions. I appreciate your support and guidance and for getting back to me so quickly each time I had an inquiry!

Thank you to the others who investigated with me at some of these locations along the journey, including Jessica Daws, Ashley Raydon, Stacey Price and Amy Padgett-McCue.

Thank you to Chad Rhoad, my publisher, for answering my anxious questions with such patience on this first-time adventure. Thank you to my editor, Rick Delaney, for cleaning up my manuscript and being the polish on the rusty product. You were both so patient and complimentary during this process.

All first-person accounts in *Haunted Atchison* are the author's personal experiences while at the location.

Introduction

History of Atchison

Nestled next to the Missouri River in Northeast Kansas is the town of Atchison. At one time, it had the most millionaires per capita in the United States, and it includes forty-two places in the National Register of Historic Places. Residents today enjoy the quiet, small-town feel of a city that has half the population it once had in the 1950s and eight times fewer than when it was the popular stop for pioneers moving west toward unsettled land or in the hopes of building a fortune. For an eight-square-mile city, it has a captivating history. The city was important in the establishment of both Kansas and America. For many pioneers headed west, they stayed in Atchison, either after falling in love with the town or because they saw the potential for building wealth as a westward supply stop. Atchison has been called the "Most Haunted City in Kansas" by many; it may be one of the most haunted cities in America. Many theories have contributed to this possible claim to fame. First is the city's significance during a time in history when many were passing through. Individuals passing through contribute to the energy of a town and leave their energetic mark. They also create an environment ripe for occurrences like crime, death on the trail or other emotional events that leave behind energy prints. Additionally, founding settlers who were displaced from other countries or traveled west from other states built their wealth from nothing. Most were hardworking immigrants who built their own homes and passed them down for generations to come. This not only leaves an energetic print on the house and town but may also create the desire to linger in the afterlife because they are so attached to the wealth they worked so diligently to create. Another element important to note is the geological vastness of limestone. Theories suggest that limestone holds energy and contributes to experiences of paranormal activity. Notable also is the Missouri River. This large body of water not only was a sought-after place to end one's life early in the town's history, but also water is considered a conductor of energy, thus increasing paranormal activity. Lastly, the removal and eventual relocation of buried residents occurring multiple times may have created such an unrest that the spirits cannot peacefully move on in the afterlife.

Kansas was named after the land's first inhabitants, the Kansa Native Americans, sometimes spelled Kanza, which means "people of the south wind." Kansa warriors were described by early explorers as "tall, handsome, vigorous, and brave." Thomas Say noted on his expedition through Kansas that, along with carefully plucked arms, chins, eyebrows and scalps except for a strip of hair down the middle adorned with an eagle or deer feather, these warriors also wore leggings, moccasins and had colorful paint on their bodies. The women of the tribe were noted to be much dowdier in appearance and responsible for doing the majority of the tribal work. The Kansa women, with their long braided hair, never complained or objected to the hard work it took to care for the family and tribe. Unlike other tribes that explorers had seen, living in communities of teepees, the Kansa tribes built sturdy grass lodges. The Kansas plains were rich with roaming buffalo, which was the main source of food and supplies for the tribe. Pierre-Jean De Smet stated of his interactions with the tribe, "The Kansa are no strangers to the tenderest sentiments of piety, friendship, and compassion." The Kansa tribe was very spiritual with earthly elements, and it is thought that they may have conducted spiritual ceremonies involving burning their enemies' hearts on Bear Medicine Island, just miles south of Atchison.

At noon on July 4, 1804, near the Santa Fe Depot located on Commercial Street, Meriwether Lewis and William Clark stopped to examine the land on their way to discover the passage leading to the Pacific Ocean. Lewis and Clark noted the deserted land of the Kansa tribe, seeing their settlement empty. They declared the name of the nearby river Independence River, to celebrate Independence Day. The Kansa had not deserted their lands. Instead, they were out hunting buffalo at the time of Lewis and Clark's visit. Eventually, the Kansa were promised new land and help by the

The corner of Third & Commercial, looking southwest. About 1869

Corner of Third Street and Commercial, looking southwest, 1869. *Courtesy Atchison Historical Society.*

government to relocate, because the government wanted to establish the area as the state of Kansas. The tribes migrated south to Oklahoma, and promises went unkept.

Just west of Atchison was Mormon Grove, a stopping point for Mormons on their journey west to Utah. The Mormon Migration followed the Mormon Trail through what would one day be Atchison. The Mormon people were moving west to seek a new settlement to practice their religion in peace. The Mormon Grove settlement was abandoned in 1849 due to a cholera outbreak that killed many of the settlers. Many of the Mormons who died of disease remained buried on the land, even though their families moved on to Utah.

Kansas, now owned by the government, was officially open for settlement. The first resident, George Million, built a house and owned a saloon near the ferry landing at the bottom of Atchison Street. He claimed 160 acres of land, which he sold for $1,000, at the time considered an inflated price, to Dr. John H. Stringfellow. Stringfellow came to Atchison with five other men from Missouri in hopes of establishing Kansas as a pro-slavery state. When the Kansas land was opened, the government decided to allow residents to determine if they would be for or against slavery. So men like Stringfellow hoped to settle the new land and sway the vote. Town leaders were soon chosen, and Atchison was mapped out by the leaders along the riverside while sitting under a large cottonwood tree half a block south of Atchison Street. One of those men, and the town's namesake, David Rice Atchison, was a Missouri senator. Interestingly, Atchison never lived in the town. Once it was established, he went back to Missouri. An 1897 news article explains that he had no interest in the town and was more interested in going back to Platte, Missouri. After the first sale of lots took place, he left and never returned. He is also a former president of the United States, although you will not see his name in any official list. His presidency lasted just one day, when Zachary Taylor refused to take the oath of office on the Sabbath. David Atchison never married. He built a 1,700-acre farm in Missouri, but his spacious mansion was destroyed by fire. His life ended in a small cottage erected on his farm in 1870.

If any town desired to grow and survive, a hotel and a newspaper were two vital enterprises. The National Hotel, at the corner of Atchison and Second Streets, was built, and J.H. Stringfellow and Robert S. Kelley started a printing office. Once the U.S. Post Office made Atchison the headquarters for all mail going west in 1855. The stagecoach line from Atchison to California was established, and soon the city was bustling with travelers headed to the promise of gold or land. The city also had one of the best steamboat landings on the busy Missouri River. With from two to five landings a day, it was a successful commercial hub. As commerce began to decline in the 1860s, the

Trains near downtown area, early 1900s. *Courtesy of Atchison Historical Society.*

Flood of White Cray Creek, 1890. *Courtesy Atchison Historical Society.*

Atchison, Topeka & Santa Fe Railroad was founded, and this ensured the prosperity of the city and its residents through the early 1900s. Judy Garland sang of the railroad in her Oscar-winning song "On the Atchison, Topeka and the Santa Fe" in the 1946 film *The Harvey Girls.*

Atchison became one of America's boomtowns. The railroad brought goods to help those citizens who wanted to plant roots in the town and allowed merchants to sell products at one of the last stops before travelers headed west. Also contributing to the boom was the immigration of Germans, who made their mark on Atchison with their cultural customs and identity. Other immigrants included the Irish Catholics, who were fleeing the potato famine and other displacement. They greatly contributed to the town's Catholic heritage. For Atchison's first thirty years, the most common language spoken was German.

Many diseases plagued the country in the early nineteenth century, and Kansas was hit especially hard. As immigrants came into the United States from countries like Ireland and Germany, they brought with them diseases never seen by Native Americans originally on American soil. As citizens

Entrance to the shopping center built after the 1958 floods destroyed the downtown buildings, 2023. *Brooke Montoya.*

migrated west, diseases spread, too. The Spanish flu was particularly deadly, killing more people than in World War I, about one-fifth the population. The first case in the United States was in Fort Riley, Kansas, in the spring of 1918. Some victims died within hours of their first symptoms; others lived a few days. Young adults were among the hardest-hit demographic. The deaths of young family members and the extensive numbers of those lost to illness contributed to the hardship experienced in Kansas during its early history.

When many people think of Kansas, they think of the movie *The Wizard of Oz*, in which Dorothy is swept away by a tornado to the Land of Oz. Interestingly, Atchison has never experienced a tornado. A force of nature that has affected the town is flooding. In 1958, two large floods of White Clay Creek occurred. The damage to the downtown area was so devastating that many buildings could not be saved. To move forward as a city, Atchison created the Urban Renewal Projects, which resulted in the outdoor shopping area downtown. The shopping area is located where Commercial Street originally existed from Fourth to Fifth Streets.

Black History of Atchison

The initial goal of residents from Missouri was to settle in Kansas and establish the state as pro-slavery. But this attempt was unsuccessful. What remained was divided residents, some for slavery, others who identified as abolitionists. One such resident, Pardee Butler, was vocal in his stance as an abolitionist, and this almost cost him his life. Reverend Butler settled in Atchison in 1855, having come from Illinois. He built a log cabin on his farm and then went into town to board the steamboat to retrieve his wife and family and bring them to their new home. During a trip into town to get supplies, Pardee Butler was overheard expressing antislavery views. He was confronted by a group of men who insisted he sign a statement in support of slavery. Pardee refused to sign. The mob dragged him to the riverbank after painting the letter *R* on his head, for "rogue." They tarred and feathered him, placed him on logs tied together and threw him into the river. They told him that the next time he came to town they would hang him. Atchison was known as the "most violent pro-slavery town in the territory," as its early settlers were adamant about solidifying Kansas as a slave state.

Despite the state being a divided ground of opposing viewpoints on slavery, Kansas was considered new frontier where freed slaves could leave the past behind and establish a new future. During elections in 1878 in Louisiana, freed slaves were threatened, assaulted and murdered to prevent them from voting. The result was the "Exodus of 1879," in which over six thousand oppressed African Americans moved west from Louisiana, Texas and Mississippi in the hopes of an open society, social justice and equality of economic opportunity. Many migrants had been promised free transportation, land, and supplies for the first year, if they moved to Kansas. This unkept promise, coined the "Kansas Fever Myth," saw no resources or support for the migrants. Newcomers heading to Kansas primarily settled in Lawrence, Topeka and Atchison.

Back when Kansas was not a safe state for people of color or those who were against slavery, it did not take evidence or the truth to punish an individual. On January 4, 1870, George Johnson was hunting and accidentally shot a white man named Mr. Cox. Johnson was arrested and held in a jail at Sixth and Santa Fe Streets. Even though Cox made a full recovery and the shooting was not intentional, a mob of fifty white men showed up at the jail, ready to take the law into their own hands. At 11:30 p.m. the mob frightened off the one deputy on duty, strung a rope around Johnson's neck and dragged him into the street. Johnson was taken to Fourth and Commercial

Streets, where the mob proceeded to sit him up and shoot several bullets into his body. Johnson did not die from the bullet wounds, so the angry mob carried his battered body to the Fifth Street viaduct. It is there the mob used the rope around Johnson's neck to hang him from the viaduct, lynching him in the streets. Johnson's widow bravely filed a lawsuit against those responsible for her husband's brutal death and won $20,000 and then quickly left Atchison.

George Johnson Memorial, dedicated in 2021, seen here in 2022. *Brooke Montoya.*

Because of the diligent research of Joshua Wolf, a Benedictine College history professor, this forgotten part of Atchison's history has been resurrected. In 2022, the City of Atchison honored George Johnson's life by holding a memorial walk. People gathered at Sixth and Santa Fe, where the jail once stood, and solemnly took the same journey Johnson did that fateful night. There is a plaque and a statue in his honor between Fourth and Fifth Streets on Commercial. George Johnson will never get justice, but his legacy will serve as a visual reminder of the racial violence that existed in Atchison's history. It is hoped that those who come across his memorial will be encouraged to honor George Johnson and learn about the city's stories that deserve to be known.

Around 1890 near White Clay Creek between Eleventh and Tenth Streets was a part of town known to residents as Happy Hollow. It was named for a Black church located there. The area comprised approximately seventeen houses and fifty people of color. Rosa Smith was a Happy Hollow resident, almost a centenarian, who wished to die while worshiping Jesus. One day, after walking to church and leading the singing, she kneeled to pray. After she did not move for some time, someone went to check on her. She had in fact died during the worship service. Another resident, King Herod, was the sage of the area. Residents paid him a percentage of their weekly wages for his wisdom and advice. Jake Williams and Jordan Coleman were avid gardeners who competed each spring for the best produce. A tune often sung in the "Hollow" for years was about the story of Riley Highbaugh, who went out to shoot a hog but missed completely and shot Lim Johnson in the eye. Fortunately, Lim lived, but Riley became the subject of the beloved rhyme, "Riley put three shots in Lim Johnson's eye." Near the railroad tracks between Tenth and Eleventh Streets was another area of town predominately

Black citizens of Atchison participating in the Corn Carnival Parade, early 1900s. *Courtesy Atchison Historical Society.*

comprising people of color, Tin Town. The residents named this part of Atchison after the waste tin and tin cans dumped in White Clay Creek. Another predominately Black part of town was north of Division Street. Because of segregation, this was deemed the "Black side of town."

One of the oldest residents, Mrs. Waters, was honored in the paper when she passed in 1925. She attended the African ME Church, located then at 715 Atchison Street, organized in the summer of 1868. Because of segregation, the Black residents of Atchison attended Lincoln High, at 700 South Fourth Street. The school began in 1921 and hosted students through eighth grade. In September 1955, Lincoln School became the first school in the community to comply with the *Brown v. Board of Education* decision to end segregation in the schools.

Originally named Division Street to acknowledge the line separating city and countryside, the street's name took on a new meaning with the growing Black community in Atchison and racial segregation. In 2020, the deaths of George Floyd and Ahmaud Arbery, brought boiling frustrations of racial inequality to the surface. Three teenagers from Maur Hill–Mount Academy accomplished what others had tried to do for three decades. Division Street was renamed to Unity Street. Sophia Hill, Kennedy Kelley and Alice McConnell Curry bravely went before the Atchison City Commission and shared testimonies gathered from members of the Black community. With the support of Mayor Abby Bartlett, five hundred signatures and over fifty letters from community members, the city commission unanimously voted in favor of the name change. This symbolic change is hopefully only the beginning.

Paranormal Ripeness

Atchison's geology may hold an important key as to why it has such high levels of paranormal activity. The city was established on the banks of the Missouri River, and water is thought to be a conduit for spiritual energy, and areas near water tend to have higher levels of paranormal occurrences. This large river may partly be why the city is one of the most haunted in Kansas. Additionally, the vast limestone deposits are theorized to hold energy while also increasing paranormal communication. Many paranormal enthusiasts have considered limestone to be capable of holding residual energy, and many locations with natural limestone have high levels of paranormal activity. This idea, which has yet to be scientifically proven, is called the "Stone Tape Theory," based on a 1972 movie of the same name that attempted to explain how this can occur. Limestone quarries once thrived here. Many of the basements and foundations of homes are made of limestone. In some instances, an entire home or building is constructed with the off-white stone.

The location's historical significance may lend to its hauntings. Many of the early settlers were Irish and German immigrants either displaced from their homeland or seeking the promise of America's freedom. Others migrated from previously settled states. The ability to purchase large plots of land was available west of the overpopulated cities, allowing a family to build financial stability and, potentially, great wealth. Many early settlers grew very wealthy by providing supplies to travelers passing along the trails. Others profited from the businesses, law practices and medical facilities they owned that provided services to the residents. Many who created their wealth lived in the same home until they died and then passed the home down to future generations of the same family. The homes are vessels of memories, love, passion and sometimes tragedy. These ties to the city and their homes may be enough that the spirits never want to leave. But the city also saw hundreds of people passing through daily, and this makes the location full of vagrant energy. This is the energy of people who were searching for more and taking risks to find it in their travels. The city was also part of the Wild West, where those passing through committed crimes of opportunity. All of these factors come together in the perfect storm of lingering energy to make Atchison one of the most haunted cities in America.

Atchison grew quickly, resulting in early city planning not being efficient. As described in more detail in the last chapter of the book, residents were buried on the outskirts of town. But what was once outskirts quickly needed to be used for new homes and more development. This happened several times until official cemeteries were established that remain today. Unfortunately, previously buried individuals were moved to new plots more than once. Some were completely left behind. This upheaval likely did not allow the souls of the dead to rest. This regretful piece of the city's history may be an important element of why so many spirits still linger.

A current resident told me about a friend of theirs who was a psychic medium. The psychic medium fell in love with Atchison, as many do. However, the individual eventually had to move. The spirit energy was so strong it made them unwell. This individual lived on Santa Fe Street and described the ghostly energy as a wave of spirits passing by daily. The ghosts bombarded them daily and would not allow them to rest. This is the feeling I have of Atchison. There is something about this beautiful town that draws you in, but spiritual energy lingers everywhere. Much like the social events the affluent attended in the past, often reported on in newspapers, residents seem to visit one house to the next in the afterlife as well. The geology, history and cemetery upheavals create a unique combination, making the town ripe for paranormal activity.

1

ZIBOLD-HAEGELIN BREWERY

PAST CLOSING TIME

Located at Tenth Street and Price Boulevard on the southwest side of the city, a bustling brewery provided Atchison residents with a sense of community and made national history. The brewery stretched the entire span of land from the east side of Price Boulevard to the other side of the creek, where Bromley Park is now. It had seven buildings, including a beer garden for drinks and entertainment. The owners, Josef Haegelin and Herman Ziebold, both emigrated from Germany and served up a popular brew, Home Favorite. An 1880s map of Atchison and a few protected photographs are all that physically remain of this remarkable location, but there might be more that lingers past closing time, waiting on that last serving of beer.

It is important to note that after immigrating, Herman changed the spelling of his name from Ziebold to Zibold. In articles and city directories, his first name is spelled a variety of ways, including Herman, Herrman and Hermann. On his gravestone, his name is spelled Herman Zibold. There are also various spellings of Josef Haegelin's name, including Joseph Hagelin, but his gravestone has Joseph F. Haegelin. Both men and their families are buried at Mount Vernon Cemetery. For simplicity, we will refer to the men based on the spelling of their gravestones.

Joseph became an experienced maltster working for Henry Nunning Brewery in St. Joseph, Missouri. It was there he met Herman Zibold, the foreman of the brewery and also an immigrant from the same town as Joseph. Herman's younger sister Emma was a courageous young woman who came to Atchison by herself as soon as she turned of age. Herman introduced Joseph to Emma, and the two married, making Herman and Joseph brothers-in-law.

Ready to plant roots and start a family, Joseph and Emma visited Atchison and were amazed by its beauty. Joseph said the steep bluffs reminded him of his hometown in Germany. Honing his malt-making skills, he took a job as a foreman with the leading brewer in Atchison at the time, Frank Young. The Young Brewery was located where Trinity Lutheran Church currently stands at Eighth Street and Laramie Street. The German population was growing quickly, and so was the demand for beer, Germany's national drink. Joseph called his brother-in-law, and together they bought A. Stern's Brewery on Price Boulevard in 1871. The Zibold-Haegelin Brewery was born!

The brewery grew and became one of the largest in the city. Bands from all over came to play music, and residents hosted social parties at the venue. A pond next to the brewery became an ice-skating rink during the winter, and the trolley car transported patrons to and from the Taylor Race Track, also on the southwest side of town.

Unfortunately, talk of prohibition was growing, and the liquor traffic laws of Kansas were making it more difficult to operate the brewery. In

The Zibold – Haegelin, "Atchison Brewery"

The Zibold-Haegelin Brewery consisted of seven buildings and spanned the area of Tenth Street and Price Boulevard, circa 1910s. *Courtesy Atchison Historical Society.*

1879, Kansas became a "dry state," meaning the sale of any liquor or beer was now illegal. Joseph, known as a stubborn man, would not accept that ruling, so he and Herman took their case to keep the brewery open to the U.S. Supreme Court. This decision made the brewery nationally famous. Although the Supreme Court sided with the State of Kansas, the brothers-in-law had Governor J.A. Martin and the sheriff on their side. Maybe Martin felt that he owed the men. A story is told that Herman Zibold saved Martin's life when both were soldiers in the Civil War. As a nod to liquor laws, Martin would have Herman "arrested" by having the sheriff pick him up as though he was upholding the law, but Herman never actually went to jail. Instead, he would take Herman to the sheriff's house, hang out for a few hours and then return him to the brewery.

Joseph and Emma lived at 936 Price Boulevard in a large, red-brick home with grapes growing on the terrace. Just north of Joseph was Herman Zibold's house. Both houses were positioned directly across the street from the brewery. Herman and his wife, Rosa, had several children. Their daughter Louisa eventually married Dr. Charles C. Finney. Dr. Finney, the son of M.C. and Kate Finney, grew up at the property on North Second Street infamously known as the Sallie House.

Around 7:00 p.m. on a windy April night in 1883, Herman's house caught fire. The wind blew the flames, spreading them to Joseph's house. Luckily, the fire department came quickly and saved the brewery and most of the Haegelin home, but Zibold's home was a total loss. But within a month, Adam Dilgert, a local stonemason and regular customer at the brewery, was commissioned to begin rebuilding both homes. Dilgert has an even deeper, more sinister connection to the brewery (see Chapter 9).

Joseph was a talented violinist and vocalist. People described him as friendly, but also jealous and stubborn. Joseph and Emma often entertained guests by singing, but once, when a guest asked Emma to dance, Joseph became enraged and forbade her to ever return to the brewery's garden. On another occasion, his parish priest disliked the way Joseph arranged the music in the choir during service. Joseph was so upset and so wanted control that he never returned to church and stopped practicing his faith.

Herman Zibold died suddenly in the summer of 1891 at age fifty-four in his home. He was a large man, weighing 350 pounds, so his casket had to be moved out of the home through a large window. While being carried, the handles of the casket fell off and bounced down the church steps. Just two years later, Joseph, died in his home at only forty-six years old after an infected knee worsened. The widows, Emma and Rosa, continued to run the brewery until 1902, when Kansas enforced prohibition laws. Emma turned the brewery into the Crystal Ice Company, employing her sons, August, Joseph Jr. and Karl. Around 1915, Karl bought his mom out of the company and eventually sold the seven buildings to Charles E. Pitts. In 1939, the buildings were demolished as a result of unpaid taxes.

Emma died in the home at eighty years old in 1928, passing away just days before Christmas. Interestingly, Emma's son August lived in the Herman Zibold home at 1005 Price Boulevard until he died of a stroke while watching the John F. Kennedy funeral on November 27, 1963.

The brewery buildings no longer stand. I drove to various locations to investigate this property. I investigated near the homes of the brewers, which you will read more about in Chapter 2. I also investigated Bromley Park. While at the park, I captured some interesting words on my ghost word generator, including *Frank, farmer, supplier* and *carrier*. Theoretically, the ghost word generator can be manipulated by ghosts to communicate via a large word bank. Out of these words, *Frank* stood out the most. Joseph Haegelin had a brother named Frank from St. Joseph who was present at the time of Joseph's passing. Additionally, Zibold and Haegelin were suppliers of beer. During another investigation with my team, API of Oklahoma, we were in contact with Emma Haegelin, but she is more closely connected to the family home, which is also discussed in the next chapter. If you are in the area, don't be surprised to experience the sound of music, the clinking of beer mugs, or the sounds of laughter through the whispers of the trees.

2

Price Boulevard

The Love Quadrant

This story happened in the glamorous decade of the 1980s in the house nestled on top of the hill at 936 Price Boulevard. In 1989, Lawrence "Larry" Joseph Sarvey, the new general manager and publisher of the *Atchison Globe* who typically reported the news, became the news.

Larry Sarvey brought his family from the Big Apple to small-town Atchison for his new position with the *Atchison Globe*. The family had been in Atchison for only eighteen months when Kathy, Larry's wife, moved back to New York with the children after the court awarded her an emergency divorce. Divorce cases with children can take time, so emergency divorces are more likely when the safety of the family is at risk, as in cases of domestic violence. It has not been stated publicly why Kathy received an emergency divorce after her and Larry's fifteen years of matrimony.

Larry began a relationship with a woman he worked with at the newspaper, Sandi Heaver, who also was recently divorced. This relationship was secret to most, especially at work. Sandi had a key to Larry's house, so on July 29, when he did not answer his telephone after she tried several times to reach him throughout the day, she decided to go to his house and check on him. She was barely able to open the front door but could see Larry lying in his living room, close to the front door entryway, with two shotgun wounds to his head. Larry was dead. Although screens on the windows had been cut and the phone lines severed, no items from the home were missing. There did not appear to have been a struggle; it was as if Larry was ambushed while answering the front door. The house sits atop a hill some distance from other homes, which may explain why no neighbors reported hearing anything between the hours of 2:00 a.m. and 12:30 p.m. the next day, which is when police suspected the murder occurred.

Larry's friends reported to police he had made a recent trip back to New York City where he had interviewed for a new job and hoped to rekindle his relationship with Kathy. Sandi was pregnant with Larry's child at the time of his murder, which put suspicion on her as a suspect. Perhaps she was upset and knew of his intentions to go back to his family in New York. She did have a key, and partners are often the first to be ruled out during an investigation. However, the only suspect ever investigated was Lloyd S. Heaver, a long-haul trucker and Sandi's ex-husband. He was eventually arrested. As the investigation proceeded, charges against him were dropped due to a lack of evidence. The police department's theory was that Lloyd killed Larry in a jealous rage. However, the necessary evidence to prove the case could not be obtained. Thus, Lloyd was released from prison uncharged. Three days after his release, he was seen dancing at a hotel bar with a woman of interest. Eight months later, they married. Kathy, Larry's ex-wife, became the new Mrs. Lloyd S. Heaver. Police were unsure if Kathy and Lloyd met during Larry's trial or if they had a prior relationship, likely connected to their ex-spouses' affair. But police believed that they had the right man in Lloyd. Some members of Larry's family even think that Kathy was an accomplice.

Sandi went on to have Larry's daughter, who now has a baby girl of her own. If Lloyd is guilty, we may never know, because he died in March 2009. Larry Sarvey's body was taken back to New York and laid to rest. His death is still a cold-case murder.

Although it looked much different then, Larry's house is the original home of Joseph and Emma Haegelin, who also both died there. Interestingly, Larry's middle name is Joseph. In the 1940s, another family, not strangers to tragedy, lived in the home. Mr. and Mrs. Bert Gerrish lost their first child at the age of one in the home on Price Boulevard. Additionally, Bert's sister, Mrs. John Dye, was pregnant when she slipped and fell on the wintery ice. She was only twenty-six years old when both she and her unborn child passed away due to the fall, leaving her two other children motherless. Bert's other sister also died young, at thirty-two, after a weeklong illness, leaving behind a husband and four young children, all under the age of nine. Bert took care of his ailing mother, who perished in his home, making a total of four documented deaths at Price Boulevard. The Gerrishes are buried in Oak Hill Cemetery, and Mrs. Dye and her husband are buried in Mount Vernon Cemetery. Because of the nature of

The house that was once Joseph and Emma Haegelin's home, and the location of the Larry Sarvey murder, currently is being remodeled, 2023. *Brooke Montoya.*

Mrs. Dye's last name, young people of the town have begun the lore that if you look at the family's tombstone, you will soon die.

This house is currently vacant and under renovation. As soon as I saw the home, I could feel the eeriness of its history. The fact that it stands vacant only adds to the ominous energy. While I was conducting my research, a neighbor told me that the house was purchased by a local resident. I attempted to get in touch with this person but was unsuccessful. We did investigate the area near the house and got interesting results. While blindfolded and unaware of the location where we were parked, Tammy Christine, a team member of API and a psychic medium, connected with a female who was described as being dressed beautifully with two girls near her side. She was standing outside a home and had other children as well. Tammy Christine described the location as like a children's home, as she was trying to make sense of all the other children being present that did not belong to the woman. Tammy explained that she has her children, but then she has these other children she loves that aren't her biological kids. Tammy Christine also got the name *Emma*. What is interesting about this is

Shown here is 936 Price Boulevard. Emma Haegelin stands outside the family home with the dog, 1910s. *Courtesy Atchison Historical Society.*

when you read the full story of the Zibold and Haegelin Brewery and their families, Joseph and Emma lived and died in this home. Herman and Rosa Zibold were part of the Haegelin family because Emma was Herman's sister. With the two families living next door to each other and with the brewery directly across the street, both homes were likely open to all of the children. It is likely that Emma cared for her nieces and nephews, as did Rosa with Emma's children. Tammy Christine also said that the two girls next to the woman grew up and went to a Catholic school. I have tried to confirm this but have not located evidence, although this is likely, as the family was Catholic. Additionally, right across the highway, then just a field away from the Price Boulevard home, lies Mount St. Scholastica, an academy for girls. In 1863, a small community of Benedictine nuns came to Atchison from Minnesota to establish the convent and school.

There are also many reports of the old newspaper building being haunted by a publisher who died of "mysterious circumstances," according to several sources. Could this be the ghost of Larry still trying to do his duties at his new employer? Many paranormal reports have happened there, including a locked door opening and closing by itself and typewriter noises being heard.

3

JACKSON PARK

PARANORMAL PLAYGROUND

During sunny weather, it is common to see Jackson Park full of locals strolling along the walking paths, enjoying a picnic, playing Frisbee golf, or birdwatching in the one-hundred-acre park. The park was expanded in the early 1900s by prominent citizen and public official Zaremba E. Jackson, for whom the park is named. But when night falls, this picturesque park turns into something more ominous, and you may experience the ghost of Molly.

Many locations have similar legends, and Molly in Atchison is no different. Some say she was a teenager out on a date after prom who was murdered when she would not have sex with her boyfriend. Others say Molly was once an enslaved woman whose master lynched her in a tree to punish her for seducing a man. Yet another story tells of Molly being left by her boyfriend after a fight and hanging herself from a tree out of sadness. None of the stories can be verfied, which makes them similar to legends told around campfires in other cities. Park-goers have reported seeing a full-body apparition of a woman hanging from the tree, located at the back of the park. Others have seen her walking sadly among the trees. People have reported being touched, pulled on or grabbed by something that is not visibly there. Maybe it is Molly.

Another death in the park that might lend to its haunting activity is that of Perry Johnson. Perry lived in Atchison most of his life and had once been employed as a foreman of the Rounds Lumber Yard. He lost his job with coal dealer Chas Crawford and was unable to find new employment.

An old postcard that portrays the entrance of Jackson Park, circa 1910s. *Courtesy Atchison Historical Society.*

Perry, married with a six-year-old son, lived near the park on Tenth Street, also near the Zibold-Haegelin Brewery. He was known to have a drinking problem and had recently separated from his wife after he threatened to kill her in a drunken rage while brandishing a kitchen knife. Fortunately, she escaped before Perry could harm her. According to the *Atchison Globe*, on April 9, 1895, Perry Johnson took a large dose of laudanum and hanged himself on a tree inside the park. Maybe Perry's ghost still roams the park longing after his wife.

Another story may lend to the park's haunting environment. W.J. McLaughlin's eighteen-month-old baby died near the park. The mother of the child left the baby in the home while she went out to tend to the garden. Unfortunately, the baby found a box of matches and somehow set the home on fire. The baby was unable to be rescued and burned to death in the home, located by the park. It is not known what the mother was tending to in the winter, why the baby was left alone or how a young child under two could light a match. The story is certainly mysterious.

A winding path that seems to be heading to an expanded park area but surprisingly winds and goes on for quite a long way can be explored by car. Having never been on the path before, I began to wonder if I should turn around and head back, as it was getting dark and I wasn't sure where the path led. I was worried I would reach a dead end and not have room to turn around, as the road begins to climb and the sides are steep. My word generator app showed the words *decide now.* I was unsure if this was an ominous warning or an encouragement to move forward. Unsure of how to turn around, I drove forward and then, to my surprise, I came to an elevated overlook where I could park and see the Missouri River bridge lit up. It was a beautiful view in a dark, desolate park.

On a social media post in an Atchison group, someone recently asked if others knew about the ghost of Molly. The post got over forty-two comments, many reporting hearing a woman scream or witnessing a ghostly head floating across the night sky. According to residents, the location known as Molly's Hollow is no longer accessible and is private land. But many still enjoy visiting the park at night on the slight chance they might experience an encounter with Molly or feel her grab them in the dark of the night.

4

SANTA FE DEPOT

TRAGEDY ON THE TRACKS

One can't help but notice the Santa Fe Depot when entering Atchison. The train depot stands in the middle of town on the popular Tenth Street. Erected in 1880, the two-story building is constructed in limestone and houses the Atchison Historical Society, the Atchison Chamber of Commerce, the Atchison Visitors Center and the Atchison County Historical Museum, with exhibits on the first indigenous tribes of Kansas, Amelia Earhart, Lewis and Clark, Jesse Stone and an extensive military weapon collection. The building also proudly boasts the world's smallest "unofficial" presidential library exhibit. David Rice Atchison, the man for whom the city is named, was U.S. president for one day, because the incoming president did not want to take the oath of office on the Sabbath. The building was added to the National Register of Historic Places in 2001.

Steamboats brought patrons to the city to start their journey west, and then the development of the railroad changed America and the town immensely. Trains not only transported people in ways stagecoaches couldn't, but they also delivered freight, allowing Atchison to become an affluent commerce town. When the depot was built, a number of other large and elegant buildings were being constructed to form the commerce area of the city. The facility at Tenth Street was a freight depot, where goods were delivered. The depot for passenger trains was east of this location. The parking lot of the depot used to have an old oak tree, a symbolic piece of history spanning the city's creation, and a roundhouse associated with the depot.

Left: Atchison Santa Fe Freight Depot, 2023. *Brooke Montoya.*

Below: The Santa Fe Train Depot is at the bottom of this picture of the city facing northwest toward the Missouri River, 1913. *Courtesy Atchison Historical Society.*

Four deaths associated with the depot happened in 1863 near the roundhouse at the infamous oak tree, which has long since been removed. Today, a Taco John's stands just south of the depot parking lot. The lot holds more than just retired train cars for viewing and a taco restaurant. This is where the "hanging tree" once stood. The site holds secrets of a darker time, when law and order did not exist and outlaws were a threat to citizens' welfare.

It was a hot summer day when the Sterling Gang was out looking for quick money and happened upon a boy on a farm in the western part of the county. The boy would not divulge where his mother's jewelry and money were located. Out of anger, the gang hanged him. Joe Hilton, an Atchison citizen, heard of the boy's death and held a meeting at Fourth and Commercial Streets, urging people to help him take revenge on this terrible act. The vigilance committee was created, consisting of Asa Barnes, Sandy Corbin, George Fairchild and Joe Hilton. A news article from *The Atchison Daily Champion* states the committee captured three of the four Sterling gang members, Sterling and two men of his gang, but the fourth "Pony" McDonald escaped. But John Kingston, owner of the Farm, a popular Atchison brothel, ran across McDonald in Geary City and tricked him into returning. Kingston told McDonald that if he came back to identify Sterling and the other men, he would be freed of any charges and released. McDonald agreed to return, snitched on his gang by identifying them and was prosecuted anyway. A trial was held. The men were found guilty and sentenced to be hanged from the large oak tree. Sterling was the first sent to his demise. He was placed in a wagon with a noose around his neck. The rope was tied to the oak tree. While the rope was being adjusted, Sterling was asked if he had anything to say. He replied in true outlaw fashion, "Not a word. Pull the rope. You can't make me blubber. I'm the best damn man in Kansas." The large crowd proceeded to watch more than one hundred men pull the wagon from under each outlaw until life left their bodies. The vigilance committee felt this was a good lesson of justice for lawbreakers, and it was reported that citizens lived in peace afterward. A website documenting Kansas lynchings by county shows that six members of the gang were hanged: William Sterling, Porter Sterling, Alexander Brewer, Daniel Mooney, Henry "Pony" McCartney and Edward Gilbert. So it is unclear from the newspaper article which is the true account and which Sterling brother was quoted prior to being hanged. There are reports of people seeing the ghosts of the Sterling Gang in the Santa Fe yards near the old tree as far back as the late 1800s, shortly after this happened.

While investigating this location, I had my teammate with API, Tammy Christine, blindfolded to see what information she could pick up without knowing where we were. My other teammate, Jill Stokes, was reading out the words provided by the ghost word generator. When we pulled in, we got the words *not brave*. Then Tammy Christine saw in her mind a female standing in a window holding a candle on a holder and looking worried, as if she was waiting for someone to come. Then we got the word *murder*. Tammy Christine saw a two-story porch with a tree, and the lady kept saying, "My baby, my baby." She was looking for an intruder, and it was as if she had contacted the police to help her. This is interesting, as it seems to be connected to

The Taco John's stands at the location of the Sterling Gang hanging, 2023. *Brooke Montoya.*

the hanging of the boy that resulted in the hanging deaths of the Sterling Gang. Tammy Christine seemed to be connecting to the aftermath, when the mother discovered her son was missing or dead and she was reaching out for help. We were parked facing the Taco John's, in the parking lot of the historical society. When I drove closer to the depot building, it was as if the energy was so strong that it followed me. Tammy Christine felt the energy become angrier and more aggressive. Tammy Christine saw a swing set at a school and feet running as if someone was being stalked. Maybe this is connected, maybe she was picking up on a different incident in the area or maybe she was picking up on Sterling himself.

Another legendary story concerns Britt Craft, one of the best train engineers, who died a hero because of a quick decision he made on a summer night in 1882. Craft, an Atchison resident, was navigating his train four miles north of Cawker City. Unbeknownst to him, a bridge ahead was on fire. He was eventually forced to decide between continuing over the burning bridge or slamming on his brakes. He decided on the latter and stopped as quickly as he could, which sent the train tumbling into the creek below. Surprisingly, all of the passengers walked away from the train derailment, but Craft was thrown from the train and killed instantly. A seven-foot memorial located in Mount Vernon has an ornate train carved into the stone to commemorate his heroic act. However, Britt continued to take his job seriously, and his death was not the end of his time as an engineer. The burnt bridge was rebuilt, and when the first passenger train passed the site of the derailment, a train's steam whistle could be heard by the conductor. Leaning out the window to look, he saw a white, transparent apparition of Britt Craft, as if sitting in the conductor's seat. The man exclaimed to all who would listen, "I've seen the ghost of Britt Craft!"

William Bouler would normally be a castoff in society in the early 1900s, but his determination in the face of his circumstances is a story bigger than his boots on display at the Atchison Historical Society Museum. At the Tenth Street railroad crossing, William "Willie" M. Bouler, or "Deafy," as he became affectionately known, lost both of his legs below the knees after a train accident. Deafy, born deaf and mute, became a bricklayer and contributed greatly to the original paved streets of Old Atchison. Despite his limitations, he never complained and was deemed the fastest bricklayer in the world. The run-in with the train wasn't the only tragedy that Deafy survived. On March 8, 1900, Bouler and his friend Leonardi, also deaf and mute, were riding in their horse-drawn buggy to the island across from the Soldier's Orphan's Home. Their buggy attempted to cross a sheet of ice, but the ice broke, and the buggy turned over, knocking the men into the muddy water below. Both being mute, they could not call for help. Two citizens happened to pull up and see the men. Stuck for over thirty minutes in freezing water and with no legs to help him swim, Deafy narrowly escaped death. His contribution to the beauty of Atchison will live on, as a city ordinance prevents the original brick roads from being destroyed or paved over. He was coined "the most fascinating man in Kansas." His gravestone is a remarkable site and can be viewed in the Mount Vernon Cemetery. Some of the activity the depot experiences might be Deafy coming to check on his boots in the museum.

Bill "Hangman" Fields was a fearless and dedicated railroad worker. He got his nickname because of his unusual way of hanging onto the freight as it was hoisted into train cars. Passersby would often get a wave from Bill as he hung high above the railway, happily doing his job. Unfortunately, while Bill was working with a large load of freight, the rope he was hanging from snapped, and he fell and was crushed by the freight. Some hear footsteps and what might be Bill still working the job he loved in an area of the building that no longer has a second floor. With the number of historical items in the museum, it is no surprise that the depot is the site of experiences that cannot be logically explained and might be of another realm. Museums often hold items so precious that it is hard for people to part with them in the afterlife. Additionally, people may be experiencing energetic remains exhibited as paranormal. I theorize that spirits come and visit their prized possessions when they choose.

5

RIVERHOUSE STEAKHOUSE, PAOLUCCI'S DELI, LOPEZ DE MEXICAN AND PETE'S STEAKHOUSE

LINGERING LUNCH-GOERS

RIVERHOUSE RESTAURANT, 101 COMMERCIAL STREET

One of the oldest buildings in Atchison, this upscale steakhouse is a go-to location for date night and Sunday brunch. It was reopened in 2021, and owner Kathleen Mayer has poured her energy into bringing this place back to life. Located next to the Missouri River, the two-story, 16,300-square-foot restaurant has an outdoor patio for those perfect spring days and summer nights. Previously, this location was the headquarters for the Atchison & Nebraska Railroad. In 1887, the building was turned into a brothel hotel when it was purchased by Ella Donoghue. The building also housed the Rotary Club of Atchison and once was the firehouse. It was eventually converted into the restaurant the Hoof and Horn before becoming Riverhouse Steakhouse.

According to the city's haunted tour conducted during the Halloween season, in 2007, a guest was eating at the Hoof and Horn and asked the server if the site had any ghosts. The server revealed that there is a female ghost that likes to hang out in the ladies' restroom. The server said she had never seen the ghost but did experience a mirror fly off the wall and breaking, and a cell phone fly off a table and soar across the room. A customer with psychic abilities was dining at the restaurant for her birthday when she went upstairs to use the restroom. While washing her

Above: 101 Commercial Street, 1913. *Courtesy Historical Society.*

Left: Riverhouse Restaurant on Commercial Street, 2022. *Brooke Montoya.*

hands, she felt the energetic presence of something that made her quickly look up. Behind her in the mirror she saw the face of a woman. In the book written by the chamber of commerce, a past manager of the restaurant was working late doing the payroll when the lights went off and nobody was near the switch. The manager was so freaked out by the negative energy in the basement that they would never go down into it, even with other people. The one time they did go down into the basement, the energy was negative and drove them to tears. Another manager reported having to consistently change the light bulb over the basement stairwell because it would regularly shatter, and employees would frequently hear footsteps upstairs when no one else was there.

While eating at Paolucci's Deli, I met Geneeka Ross, a waitress who had worked at the Riverhouse. I asked her if she had ever had personal experiences there. With eyes wide, she replied, "Oh yes! That place is very haunted!" She described the vision of a woman that others also reported seeing lingering on the patio steps at night. She also heard footsteps in the basement. She has witnessed apparitions captured in pictures that others have shown her taken at the restaurant. Nobody seems to have identified who the mysterious ghostly woman is, but she has been seen by many.

Paolucci's Restaurant Deli + Lounge, 115 South Third Street

Paolucci's Restaurant has been owned by the same family and in the same location since it began in 1894, when two brothers, Felix and Dominic Paolucci, moved to Atchison from Italy. Dominic and his wife, Rosa, started Paolucci's Grocery. It quickly became one of the largest grocery stores in town. This was the first restaurant my paranormal investigation team ate at when visiting Atchison to investigate the Sallie House. We had connected with another team in Kansas that wanted to meet for dinner, and we had seen this location on a few websites, where it was listed as being "haunted." My favorite meal is the chicken tender basket with gravy, but they have many dishes I have yet to explore. The Paoluccis emigrated from Italy, so the menu highlights specialties like Paolucci's Italian Dinner and the Taste of Italy. The business comprises three sections. The restaurant has tables and booths for dining, and the deli sits next to it with an adjoining walkway. On the second floor is a lounge area. Next to the deli is a banquet room that guests can rent for parties or special occasions.

The current owner, Margie Begley, explained to me that upstairs is where the Paolucci family lived. Dominic and Rosa had four children, boys Nick, John and Felix and a girl, Mary. Mary was born in a house across the alley near the restaurant. The children helped in the family business and grew up to have families of their own. Felix moved away to join the navy. In 1936, Mary married a man named Ed Begley and created the Paolucci & Begley Grocery. Together, they had four children, Rosemary, Ed, Joe and Mike. Nick married and had two children. Tragically, Nick's wife and child died in the same year, and within a short time Mary lost her husband, Ed, to a ruptured appendix. Brother and sister became even closer and raised their children together.

In the early years, Nick often stayed upstairs. For a long period, the upstairs lounge was also known as the Old Traveler's Hotel and rented

Left: Members of Afterlife Paranormal Investigations of Oklahoma having dinner at Paolucci's with local paranormal investigators. *Back row, left to right*: Stephanie O'Reilly, Rhonda Constant, Wayne Holt, Andy Hartman, Brooke Montoya, Jessica Daws and Amy Padgett. *Front row, left to right*: Amy Holt, Amanda Coots, Tammy Christine and Jill Stokes, 2021. *Brooke Montoya.*

Below: Paolucci's Restaurant, Deli & Lounge, 2023. *Brooke Montoya.*

rooms to people passing through. Margie shared with me that several paranormal investigation teams have visited the location over the years and reported communicating with and seeing what was likely Nick and brother John upstairs. This is also where the staff tends to have unusual experiences. A previous bartender shared a story on their YouTube channel, Dreaming of Diamonds. She said that she never saw anything but heard voices when nobody else was around late at night while cleaning. She also had coworkers tell her that they saw the full apparition of a man many times. Margie spoke of another theory as to who the man could be. Margie thinks the man may have been a longtime renter when the space was a hotel. Geneeka Ross, a waitress working there, happily shared with me that she hears unusual sounds and her name being called by a female voice. She works in the restaurant area where these incidents occur. She also shared a story of a young boy who went into the restaurant bathroom and came out frightened because it was freezing cold and the water came on by itself. I giggled to myself, thinking of Mrs. Paolucci in spirit being motherly and turning the water on to remind the boy to wash his hands. While walking through the location, I found that the women's bathroom also has a lot of energy. Maybe it is the antique pictures that remind me of my grandma, as she had the same framed pictures of a boy reading a book and a little girl having a tea party hung on her walls. Or maybe I am picking up on the nearby men's bathroom, but the area is heavier. Additionally, Margie had me walk in the banquet room, and I experienced energy heavier toward the back. After I told her what I was feeling, she explained that people have experiences in that area of the building as well.

The site is more than 128 years old, and the building is one of the only structures to survive the two devastating floods in 1958. The history of the Paolucci and Begely families lives on through Margie. Mike, her husband, passed away a couple of years ago. As Margie was telling me about Mike, I felt chills around my body as if he was there, running the restaurant with her. She said she does not experience things in the building, but she explained that she may not be paying as much attention or be as open to it as other people are. She did say that every once in a while she acknowledges her husband when she finds something she was looking for or something funny happens.

LOPEZ DE MEXICO RESTAURANT, 112 SOUTH SIXTH STREET

Having visited this restaurant while in town a few times, I got a sense that the location had stories, and I was not wrong! Located in the heart of downtown by the Sixth Street viaduct, this building has seen several businesses over the years. The earliest tenant that can be identified is R.H. Biezard, a gunsmith whose business fitted keys, repaired locks and more, in 1888. After this, it was the business of Adams Bros. & Hamm, which was changed to Jay D. Adams. The firm conducted loans, real estate and insurance. Sometime after 1931, it became Hilligoss Shoes. This store was established by Edward Hilligoss and is now a few doors down and co-owned by his great-granddaughter Sarah Biechele and great-grandson Adam Biechele. At some point, it became Jerry's BBQ. Now it is my favorite place in Atchison to get chips and salsa, Lopez de Mexico.

Based on the restaurant menu, the history began with Enrique Lopez, who emigrated from Mexico at the age of eight. Elena Vallejo was born in Horton, Kansas, a city referred to as "Little Mexico" because of its large population of Mexican residents, who settled there to work for the Rock Island Railroad. Elena married Enrique. In Atchison, they were known as Helen and Henry. They had seven children. In 1995, they opened the Lopez de Mexico Restaurant to bring their culture to Atchison via food and music. They live by the motto of treating customers "like part of the family" and keep the restaurant within the Lopez-Vallejo family. Many of the employees have worked with the restaurant since its conception.

While my team ate at this location, we felt the energy of the space. I asked the waitress if she experienced any paranormal activity. She excitedly told

Lopez de Mexico, 2022.
Brooke Montoya.

me to wait just a bit and that she would send Anne Pruett, the owner, right over. Anne, a friendly, longtime resident, told us the story of the lady in the black dress. During the fall festivities one year, a skilled psychic working with the festival, Glennie Turner, liked to eat at the restaurant, because patrons left her alone and allowed her some psychic downtime. During one of her lunches, she called Anne over and asked her, "Who is the lady in the black dress?" Anne was uncertain whom she was referring to. Glennie told her that she had dark hair pulled into a bun and wore a long black dress and black boots, as if she was from the railroad era. Glennie informed Anne that the lady looked upset at her waitress with the red hair. Anne looked at Glennie in shock, as that waitress had recently had a negative interaction with a customer. It appeared the lady in the black dress was not happy with the way the waitress had handled the situation! Anne did not tell anyone about her conversation with Glennie except her husband, George.

One day, the sighting of the lady in the black dress was confirmed when a frequent customer was overheard by her husband talking about the woman in the black dress pacing the kitchen and continuously going out the back door. Her husband's ears perked up, having heard this story from his wife not long before. He rushed to the man and asked him what he was seeing. George admits he believes ghosts could exist but always is a bit skeptical. Not wanting to give the customer any information of what Anne had told him, George asked the customer questions to let him reveal what he saw without any help. The customer described the same woman in the black dress and boots and stated that he often sees her following the waitstaff or ushering behind the busboys as if saying, "Hurry up, clean these tables!" She seems to take great pride in the restaurant and making sure it's running smoothly. Anne's husband was excited to share with his wife what the customer told him and confirm multiple sightings of the same spirit. The identity of the lady in the black dress is not known, but Anne is thankful that this spirit keeps a watchful eye over the restaurant and wants the business to thrive by keeping the waitstaff in line.

PETE'S STEAKHOUSE, 618 COMMERCIAL STREET

Tucked among the historic commercial buildings, Pete's Steakhouse is a restaurant you do not want to miss, not only for its lingering lunch goers in spirit but also because the food may be what keeps the ghosts from not wanting to move on after death. Revekkah Tsamolias, the warm and friendly owner, blends the perfect combination of historic Atchison with her native Greece to offer a menu of amazing dishes. Opened in the 1980s by her husband, Pete, and his brother George, the restaurant is in the heart of downtown and includes a main dining area and kitchen, a second floor that is used for events and a basement used for storage.

Revekkah showed us the front entrance, to the side of the main restaurant door, where patrons used to be able to enter the basement when it was once the site of a speakeasy. The sign above the descending stairs reads "The

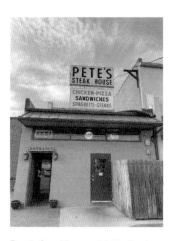

Pete's Steakhouse, 2023. *Brooke Montoya.*

Boiler Room," and the ceiling of the basement is only five feet, ten inches high, barely taller than me. The speakeasy could not be verified, but maybe that just means it was a well-hidden gem.

In the late 1800s, the building was used by the Presbyterian and Baptist churches for bake sales, festivals and other events. It also housed Farmers Bank and Reynold's Real Estate Company. Around 1911, Hill's Studio for photographs, the Busy Bee Shoe Company and the Atchison Cash Store all shared the address. The business was sold for $15,000 by D. Katz, who advertised everything at a bankrupt sale that year. Might Katz be lingering and unhappy about losing his shoe business? There is evidence that around the mid-1940s, the location was a Firestone tire store. The building was saved from demolition as part of the Urban Renewal Project in 1963 when the action was dropped and Ethel Morrissey, the owner of the building, was able to make needed repairs to keep it standing.

When I met Revekkah, I asked her if my team and I could investigate the premises, and she graciously allowed us access to the second floor and basement. Our team, API of Oklahoma, is always ready to explore. Tammy Christine, Jill Stokes and I explored the upstairs first. I was especially intrigued by the back stairs, feeling a strong pull when first entering the building. The upstairs near the restrooms was also especially strong. While upstairs, I saw in my mind's eye the image of a heavy-set, shorter man, slightly balding. He was sweeping the first floor and wearing an apron. I am not sure who he was, but I got the feeling he owned the place, potentially when it was previously a store. Tammy Christine saw a similar man. She also felt energy toward the back stairs and said, "I feel like someone fell down those stairs, but they didn't die here." To her, that meant they were likely okay but that they had fallen and were potentially hurt. We went back downstairs to ask Revekkah how to access the basement so we could continue our investigation. First, we asked Revekkah if someone had fallen down the stairs. She slowly shook her head yes. I looked at Tammy Christine, and we locked eyes in disbelief. No matter how many accurate readings you experience, it is still surprising and validating to hear confirmations about information that comes to you. I asked the owner when the person fell. She hesitated and said, "Today." I think all of us were in such shock that it was hard to process what we just heard. I turned to look at the waitstaff, who looked shaken and emotional. I asked if the person was okay, and Revekkah shook her head, revealing to us that the man had passed away only about an hour before. This news was jarring. We felt terrible for him, his family and the staff at the restaurant who had experienced this event. Tammy had picked up on the man who had fallen that very day who in fact did not die on the premises, but did later at the hospital.

We went down to the basement and were met by an employee who has worked at Pete's for almost a year. He told us of two women and a man he sees occasionally in the basement. The women are together, one in a sundress, the other in overalls. They sit together as if talking and turn to look at the employee as though he is invading their space when he comes down into the basement. The male spirit is on the other side of the basement, and the employee says he just stares at him in a threatening way. It makes him feel very uncomfortable. Tammy felt the spirit also made the female spirits uncomfortable, as if he was also encroaching on their space.

Revekkah said the lights upstairs often turn off and on by themselves, voices are heard and customers mention seeing or hearing things while dining. Revekkah laughed, affectionately telling us she has never had any such experiences, because she is too mean for the ghosts to approach her. She embraced us with welcoming arms, and you could tell the community loves her (and her food). Every guest dining that day had long conversations with her while they were eating. When you are in Atchison, make sure to come eat at Pete's. Just know that you may have some unexpected guests join your dining party.

6

MISSOURI RIVER

WATERY GRAVES

The Missouri River is what divides Kansas from the neighboring state of Missouri. The river is large, and its current is swift. It is the centerpiece in Atchison's history. The river is what allowed Atchison to have its successful commercial start with the steamboats coming north. Being the last stop before the river narrows, Atchison was the best location to exit the steamboat and move west by stagecoach for new land or golden riches. It was beside the river at the large, mangled oak tree that the founders of Atchison plotted the city's streets. Many residents established their homes alongside the beautiful river on the steep bluffs to take in its beauty. This beautiful river holds plenty of secrets, too.

On February 5, 1870, the *Weekly Atchison Champion* reported that two women, "evidently tired of this world's conflicts and strife," took their lives by jumping into the Missouri River and drowning. Only one body was recovered. The current of the Missouri River is swift and unforgiving, able to carry one away quickly before they realize what is happening. George Littleton's body was found when, on May 25, 1903, he ended his life in the river, "driven to desperation by an unsuitable marriage."

F.W. Plummer, another name associated with the river, may have ended his life in the Missouri River. It is also possible that he pulled off the biggest scam of the early 1900s. J. Botkin, an Atchison resident, found the hat of Plummer, a traveling man who had been staying at the Byrum Hotel. The hat was carefully placed with an iron span in order to keep the wind from blowing it away. Tucked inside the hat was a suicide note. None of

Plummer's clothes were found. Plummer, twenty-six, had recently left his job at Frank Dilgert's store to become a traveling salesman. The night before Botkin's discovery, Plummer and Dilgert had attended a performance at the Airdome. A happy Plummer told Dilgert that he was heading to St. Joseph to see his employer.

Dilgert noted something odd that Plummer had told him. Plummer said he wished the clouds would produce a tornado to destroy the Byrum Hotel and then all his woes would be gone. Plummer's two-month marriage was already in trouble, and his wife had returned to her parents' home. Plummer said his wife was jealous and had eyes for another man. After his outing with Dilgert, Plummer went to the Stribling barbershop to get a shave and massage. When Pummer returned from the outing and went back to the Dilgert store, Plummer complained to Mrs. Dilgert that his troubled marriage would surely cause him career failure and that people would likely need to search for him in a couple of days. After Plummer's disappearance, Frank Dilgert called Plummer's employer in St. Joseph and was informed that Plummer had been fired due to his lack of performance over the previous few months. Nobody witnessed Plummer board the train, and he was not known to drink. Was his disappearance an elaborate ruse to go somewhere else and start over? Or did Plummer do what his note said and end his life in the river? He was never located, alive or dead.

In August 1855, an enslaved Black woman owned by Grafton Thomassen drowned in the river. J.W.B. Kelley, an Atchison lawyer at the time, formed the quick assumption that the woman must have taken her life, due to the way Thomassen threatened and beat her. Thomassen was a powerful man and, with the encouragement of onlookers, fought Mr. Kelley and forced the citizens of Atchison to sign a document of resolutions that forced Kelley to leave town.

Yet another drowning in the river also holds a mystery. A lady—some say she was the daughter of a notable citizen, although this has not been confirmed—was riding her buggy down Atchison Street near the ferry entrance. It is reported that the streets were icy from wintery weather, and Atchison Street has a steep decline toward the river. Heading down the street, the woman lost control of the horses and plunged into the icy river, never to be seen again. Another story is that this woman of stature was pregnant and chose to end her life instead of facing societal shame. It seems the river was not an unlikely source of exiting this life for citizens of early Atchison.

People claim that if you are walking alongside the river, especially at night, you will hear the lady call to you as if to join her in the watery grave.

The steep hill heading down Atchison Street toward the Missouri River, where the young lady on the carriage plunged to her death, 2023. *Brooke Montoya.*

She especially calls to men who report hearing her cries. Our team API took an interesting approach to investigating this area, since it is a river. We blindfolded Tammy Christine Raydon while Jill Stokes monitored our equipment and I drove around the city. Tammy Christine had no way to know where we were driving next. While driving, I made sure to go in no particular order to the various locations. I also made sure to make extra turns. I trust my teammate, but I did not want to give her any hints as to where we were going next to ensure authenticity in responses. When we drove down Atchison Street toward the river, we got to the end of the road, and Tammy Christine said abruptly, "Wait, stop!" I pulled over near the tavern that sits on the corner of Atchison Street and the Missouri River. She explained that she was seeing a female who was splashing around. Tammy Christine then said, "The girl changed her mind. She appears to be in her mid-twenties and felt desperate. It was dark outside. She lost the love of her life, she was betrayed." On the ghost word generator, we got the words *regain* and *determination*. Still blindfolded and taken aback by how strong the energy was and the messages she was receiving, Tammy Christine inquired, "Are we near water?" The ghost word generator showed *score*. At this point, I did not answer Tammy Christine about the water, and she could not hear the word generator. She then explained that she was getting the feeling of levels of water, flowing. She saw Native American mounds nearby, and they felt disturbed and unsettled. This could be due to graves, typically buried near water, having been moved when the town was being built. She pointed to a tree nearby and said the message she was receiving was that there is a tree that is important in history and everyone ignores it. It is unknown by others how important the tree is, and it gets no acknowledgment. The large, mangled oak stands nearby. This is the tree close to where the first settlers of Atchison mapped out the city, but something about this message felt that there was another tree important to them but that the mangled oak gets all the historical acknowledgment. The female that Tammy Christine picked up on appeared to add depth to our story of the female on the buggy that plunged into the river.

7

McINTEER VILLA

MAYHEM AT THE McINTEER

D riving down Kansas Avenue toward 1301, one can't help but notice one of the largest Victorian-style mansions in Atchison, nationally known as the McInteer Villa. It was built in 1889 by saddle maker John McInteer for his wife, Alice. Having emigrated from Ireland, John had created his wealth by selling his saddles and repairing wagons in his Atchison shop, one of the last locations to get supplies before heading west. Eventually, they were able to move from their home above his shop to this beautiful new villa.

With nine documented deaths in the home, it is the perfect setting for things that go bump in the night. The large home includes a basement that spans the entire footprint of the home, with a matching attic on the third floor. The first floor includes a kitchen, dining room, parlor, living area and several other rooms. The house has two staircases, one near the front entrance of the home and the other in the back that the servants would have used to access the attic and kitchen. The current owner, Stephanie O'Reilly, has restored the home and decorated each room in Victorian decor with much care and forethought.

It is rumored that John McInteer was not allowed by the residents of Atchison to build his home on the "rich" side of town, so he was forced to the west side of town. Thumbing his nose to the city, he arranged for his front door to face the side of town where he wanted to build. So the original front door faced the Missouri River. He also made a statement with the number of stained-glass windows he installed. Many of the nice homes

McInteer Villa, 2022. *Brooke Montoya.*

in town had them in the stairwell, but John put them all around his home. They were very expensive, and he wanted the town to know that his bank account was just as large as the other wealthy residents who looked down on him. John was well known in town for his fine craftmanship in saddle making. He also owned one of the largest convention halls in Atchison, able to hold approximately two thousand guests. It included a roller-skating rink and hosted political conventions and basketball games. He also owned real estate in town.

Shortly after the couple moved into the home, Alice, John's first wife, passed away from an illness. Three years later, he married a widowed mother of three, Anna Conlon Donovan. Anna had grown up in Atchison, and her parents were well known. She briefly moved to New York, where she met Peter Donovan. They were married and had three boys, Peter Jr., Fred and Charles. When Anna came back to Atchison after her husband's untimely death, Charles was the only son who followed her. Anna's mother came to live with her after Anna's father passed away, and she died at the Villa in 1899. Two years later, John McInteer passed away of dropsy. At some point after John's death, Charles J. Conlon, a prominent attorney in Atchison and

Anna's brother, brought his family to live at the Villa. Additionally, Anna brought in boarders to rent rooms. In 1916, Anna fell ill and passed away in the primary bedroom. She was found by the nurse, who was bringing her Cream of Wheat.

Anna's son Charles Donovan was in the American Expeditionary Forces. He did not enter the military until later in life and did not serve long. He broke his arm in 1918 and while away contracted an illness, likely Spanish flu, from which he struggled to heal. He was discharged from the military and sent home. On October 11, 1922, Charles ate dinner with the family, took an aspirin, retreated to his bedroom upstairs and took his own life, putting a .22-caliber bullet in his right temple. Anna's brother Charles J. Conlon was in the home and heard the shot. He was the first to find Charles Donovan, but his nephew had died before doctors could arrive. The exact location of Charles's bedroom is not known. The newspaper articles document that he went upstairs. The current owner surmises it could be the bathrooms upstairs, which share a wall. Before the house was remodeled, the two bathrooms formed a single bedroom. These rooms are next to what is now referred to as the library, which has been decorated as a tribute to Charles and includes a mannequin in a military uniform. The library is also the easiest place to get intelligent responses from a spirit that identifies as Charles and lends a heavy and sad feeling to the space. Local newspapers often reported the events of people's lives during this time, and there were no reports of Charles going on a date, taking anyone to a dance or leaving the Villa for anything besides the military in his thirties. Charles never married and did not have children.

From 1925 to 1950, the villa was a rooming house called J.N. Arthur Apartments. In 1952, Isobel Altus "Goldie" bought the home. She was an eastern transplant from Washington, D.C., where she worked for the FBI. She also was an accomplished violinist and the youngest stenographer in the world at twelve years old. She never married. Goldie bought the beautiful house with hopes of remodeling it, but money would not allow this during her residence at the Villa. Quite eccentric, Goldie often dressed in black. As a result of Goldie's living alone in such a large house, stories began circulating that she was a witch, often leading to kids harassing her, yelling mean things at the house or vandalizing her property. It is reported that she sat in the window of the parlor in her rocking chair with a gun in her lap for protection. Goldie became ill and found a couple, the Gerardys, willing to buy the home. They wanted to pour love into the Villa, repairing it to its natural beauty. The Gerardys bought the house in 1952 but allowed Goldie

Anna McInteer standing outside the Villa near the original front door on the west side of the house, early 1900s. *Stephanie O'Reilly.*

to remain there until she passed away in her rocking chair near the front-door window in 1969. Her mother may have died in the home as well. Goldie sat dead in her rocking chair for two days until being discovered by a neighbor.

The Gerardys moved into the home in 1976. In the *Kansas City Star*, Mrs. Girardy reported seeing a shadow person by her kids' room, a woman in a white dress, a boy and a woman in a pink dress.

In 2018, Stephanie O'Reilly purchased the home from the Gerardy children. In an interview, O'Reilly jokingly told me that every owner of the home thus far has died there. The house has a love/hate relationship with Stephanie. Although she jokes that she annoys the house, my experience with her in the home while investigating it is that the house truly loves how she cares for it. The house comes alive when she is there. It does so for us as well, since we are so welcomed by O'Reilly. Of course, there may be a spirit or two that was not friendly on the earth plane and continues to be grumpy toward others, including O'Reilly.

Activity happens all over the house. My team, API of Oklahoma, has been to the home five times, most recently in May 2023, when we stayed an entire week. We have had a beach ball fall down the back stairs four times in one weekend, and then, when we stayed the week, it did not happen once. Instead, our camera fell four times. What was almost written off as a problem with the tape was then viewed from the owner's camera, which was positioned behind ours. When you watch the camera fall in slow motion, you see the tape lift up without the camera moving. We also caught the cord hanging off the camera move on its own. Of eight cameras, this is the only one that was knocked over, and it was closest to another active room, which we call the "Green Room." This room, also called "Lucy's Parlor," is where we have caught the shadow man in a picture. Others have also seen him in photographs, and he is as tall as the door frame. The living room is where Goldie's chair still sits, and people have seen it rocking on its own, have felt their hair touched if they sit in the chair and have had paranormal equipment activated.

The living room is near the front door. On the front porch, people have seen Mr. Gerardy wearing his overalls. The parlor next to the living room has had the piano played on its own. There is a small room with a bathroom off the living room. People have experienced activity here, especially in the bathroom. This room is nearest the back stairs, which has the most activity. In addition to our beach balls falling, we have caught the most electronic voice phenomena (EVPs) here. We have also had a camera cord move and experienced very intelligent interaction with our equipment when we asked questions. By the front stairs on the first floor is a small storage space where the children like to play and touch equipment. Tammy Christine saw an apparition of a child pull the curtain back when she hid there during a round of hide-and-seek. We also got confirmation from popular psychic medium Jessica Potter that this is where the women ghosts of the house like to linger. She explained that the women spirits often feel sad, because guests mostly try to interact with the men of the house. The men spirits are louder and more capable of manipulating equipment and making noises. The female spirits want their stories heard, too.

The basement is huge and very haunted, exhibiting a darker energy. The spirit in the main room, where a table is set up, enjoys lighting up equipment based on dirty jokes it likes. The dirtier the joke, the more the spirit interacts with equipment. The attic also has a lot of activity. The door opens on its own; people hear voices and a baby crying, as well as other phenomena.

The second floor is likely the most active. Although not all rooms have the same amount of activity, we have had occurrences in every room of the home. The house has its resident spirits who are always here, but, according to our experiences, several psychic mediums we have worked with and others who have investigated, the house also gets transient energies. These

Oscar, the doll that lives at the McInteer Villa, 2022. *Brooke Montoya.*

are spirits in the area that are aware of the guests coming to investigate and swing by to play, but they aren't always there. Atchison is so haunted that it isn't far-fetched to think that John McInteer's friends sometimes come by and say hello when they aren't haunting their own houses in town. The McInteer burial plot is located at Mount Calvary Cemetery.

8

HANNAH JO CUSACK

LADY OF THE GARDEN

Hannah Jo Cusack became a widow only five years after marrying J.K. Cusack in 1861. He must have been her one love, as she remained unmarried for thirty-nine years, until her death in 1905. Hannah was an Irish immigrant born in the summer of 1837. She had two sons, Thomas and William. Visiting her sister in St. Louis, Hannah fell in love with Atchison, eventually making her home at 1009 Parallel Street, a gorgeous Queen Anne two-story built in 1881. The house is approximately 2,800 square feet and has three gorgeous fireplaces and a Victorian wraparound porch that was added to the home in 1910. The land the home was constructed on once belonged to George Glick, owner of the Glick Mansion, a town attorney and, eventually, governor of Kansas.

Hannah, a milliner (someone who makes or sells women's hats), became known worldwide after her corn-husk-trimmed hats won an award at Atchison's annual Corn Carnival in 1897. Within a couple of years, Hannah's beautiful and unique hats were being requested by the wife of President William McKinley. She also filled orders for Queen Victoria and Helen Gould, a philanthropist and advocate for women's equality. A national fashion show in New York City requested a variety of Cusack's hats for an exhibit to demonstrate the "evidence of the ingenuity of the 19th-century woman of the West." Her hats also appeared in London magazines.

Not only did she have an eye and passion for fashion, but Hannah was also a generous woman. In December 1887, a man lost control of his horses. As the steeds ran wild, they crashed into a storefront. The store housed a case

Left: Hannah Jo Cusack House at 1009 Parallel Street, 2023. *Brooke Montoya.*

Right: Hannah Jo Cusack, circa 1890s. *Courtesy Atchison Historical Society.*

of Hannah's items for sale, resulting in a fifteen-to-twenty-dollar loss in her products. She filed a lawsuit to reclaim her loss, but after she became aware of how poor the man was, she dropped her lawsuit and gave him the money she was initially suing him for. Hannah certainly made her mark on the town of Atchison and brought attention to women of the West as creators and entrepreneurs. A longtime resident of the town, it is said she never left.

The current owners, Sharon and Max Berry, moved into the home on June 15, 2005. Fortunately, the previous owner kept meticulous records, pictures and a complete history of the home. In her book *Who Haunts Hannah Jo Cusack Home*, a collection of stories about her time and haunted experiences in the home, Sharon writes, "Once I walked in the home I got the feeling I was home and never wanted to leave." She felt as if the house was "pulling her in" and making her feel welcome. Immediately after Sharon and Max purchased the home, renovations began. Knowing how haunted Atchison's houses tended to be, Sharon hoped this house also had afterlife activity, but past owners and neighbors were unaware if the house was indeed haunted. She decided while painting to talk to Hannah and see if she would respond. She asked Hannah what she thought about the guest bedroom being painted peach. Sharon looked down and noticed a shiny copper penny by the paint can. This was not a sure sign of Hannah's presence, but it was peculiar at the least. Max soon found a penny inside the chandelier on their eleven-foot ceilings. A contractor found a penny in the toilet tank. Each time a penny was discovered, they were placed in a box, and Max and Sharon told

Hannah "thank you" for speaking to them. Sharon explains that she finds them often after she has been thinking about or talking directly to Hannah.

On the second night of being in the home, Sharon smelled what she thought was smoke, but after she frantically woke her husband to have him check the house, he identified it as sulfur. Then they both witnessed a black mist move down the stairs and into the guest room. This was the room the cats refused to go inside and always seemed extra cold compared to other rooms. Once while having friends over, Sharon did not mention the paranormal activity, because these friends were skeptical of such things. But, when saying their goodbyes, the guests spotted a mist floating through the living-room window and were no longer nonbelievers. Another friend, Tim, is a psychic medium. When he walked through the house, he stopped at the guest bedroom and warned Sharon not to go in that room, because it has something negative and could likely be a portal. After leaving Sharron's home, he experienced a freak car accident and spent months in a back brace. Tim felt that the spirit likely followed him home, based on strange events that started happening in his residence. Sharon also experienced an immediately lighter feeling in the guest bedroom after Tim left the house. In 2008, paranormal investigators Mary van Horn and Ernie Vine came to her home. Ernie said he sensed both a dark-haired woman and a man who smoked a pipe. They came back a few months later with psychic Glennie Turner. Glennie picked up on Hannah and said she was in the home. She also said a woman named Mary and a child named Katie were there. Glennie picked up on sadness in the guest room, saying a baby was murdered there. She also felt that Tom or Thomas was in the home, which Sharon knew was Hannah's son's name. Glennie said that Hannah is grateful for Sharon's love of the home and wants her to stay forever. The psychic explained to Sharon that Hannah sees the home as it was when she lived there, filled and decorated with her personal belongings. In a verbal account in the book, Glennie states that she was excited coming up the walkway of the home, because she saw a woman looking at her from a window and knew she was in for a spiritual connection with this home. Glennie refers to Hannah as the "lady of the garden," because she loved flowers and entertaining guests at her home.

Other experiences have involved a ghost cat that likes to play with Katie and the other living cats that reside in the home. At one point, Sharon had nine cat family members. She has seen apparitions, electronics turning off and on by themselves and more events she details in her book. In 2013, Elite Paranormal of Kansas City gave details of evidence collected in the home during an investigation. They saw a misty form of a ghost child. They had psychic Harvey Althaus conduct a remote reading. He picked up on a young girl who resides in the home and likes to be mischievous. They captured a small voice saying, "Katie." They also witnessed a door open on its own.

Sharon got her wish to live in a haunted Atchison home and has resided there for many years. She explained to me that the home still feels comforting and that she and the ghosts have found their stride and know how to coexist happily. Although Hannah's home is no longer available for tours, you can still appreciate the beauty as you drive by. You might see Hannah waving to you from the upstairs window. Hannah Jo Sheehan Cusack is buried in Mount Calvary Cemetery. If you want to experience Hannah Jo's house for yourself, you can rent the room on Airbnb for a fee per night. Are you brave enough to stay in what Sharon calls the "Portal to Hell"?

9

DILGERT HOUSE

HIDDEN SECRETS

From the outside, this white, wooden, square-frame, two-story home at 919 Atchison Street looks unassuming, but inside, the spirits are aching to be heard. Built in 1880 by German immigrant Adam Dilgert, the modest home was constructed for his wife, Mary, and children Barbara, Adam and youngest son Ferdinand, named after the senior Adam's brother. Some reports indicate that his great-niece, Frances, may have lived in the home as well, but census reports do not confirm this. Adam's great-niece was the daughter of Frank and Ida Dilgert, a popular Atchison couple who ran a confectioner's store selling candy all around the world. They built the home at 320 V Street for their daughter Frances, who ended up dying at twenty-two years old, just two years after the home was completed.

Adam was a well-respected contractor and stonemason. His limestone quarry is responsible for building the foundation of Atchison between 1886 and 1894. In 1895 and 1905, the house was expanded, doubling its original size. The house now has a kitchen, bathroom, living room, dining room and bedroom on the first floor. The upstairs includes two bedrooms. There is an attic space off the side of the stairs, and underneath the home is a large basement with several rooms. The basement is rumored to have hosted gatherings for Adam and his friends, including perhaps gambling and business meetings. Another interesting feature is the pathway to the side of the house that used to be a carriage drop-off and leads to the basement, likely to carry in goods. Adam was very close to an Atchison mayor who passed away in the 1880s, and Adam placed a commemorative headstone engraved with the mayor's name in his backyard.

Adam had a reputation for drinking. Although respected for his skills as a contractor and for being peaceful, pleasant and jolly, Adam could become angry and violent when drinking. In December 1880, Adam was in the Zibold-Haegelin Brewery celebrating the end of a construction job. It was Adam's tradition to do a shot with the construction crew as a ritual of a job completed, but he was also a frequent patron of the bar. Based on newspaper reports of the trial, witnesses claimed that Ferdinand Dilgert, Adam's brother, who also lived in Atchison, was at the bar chatting with the owner, Herman Zibold, when Adam came in and went straight to the cellar. No words were exchanged at that time between the men. Later in the evening, during the celebration with the contractors, something was said between the brothers that made Adam angry. Adam reportedly slapped his brother with an open hand, then patrons hauled a very intoxicated Adam home and into bed. Ferdinand also went home half-dazed and stated that "he did not know who knocked him down." He died in his bed a few hours later. The autopsy indicated that the cause of death could not have been a strike with an open hand, as Ferdinand had contusions on his head, a bruise on his face and a cut on his ear. The examiner claimed it had to have been a strike with a closed fist and that Ferdinand was hit multiple times in anger. During testimony, people who knew the brothers reported that Adam was angry with his brother because Adam had helped him with a task and had received no thanks in return. Adam said to a witness that he was no longer calling Ferdinand his brother. Apparently, there had always been jealousy and contention between the brothers. Adams was not convicted for his brother's death. Ferdinand may be lingering in the home, seeking vengeance.

In the early 2000s, it was said that a man who lived in the home enjoyed tinkering in the basement on projects. During a drunken state, the man fell down the basement stairs and died. Keli Adams and her brother Rob Adams purchased the Dilgert House in 2014. Keli, a medium, paranormal investigator and author of many books about the paranormal, including *Atchison, Kansas: Portal to Other Worlds*, was heavily involved in the paranormal field and fell in love with the Dilgert residence. So when it hit the market, she made it her home. Unfortunately, when we investigated the home, Keli had recently passed away from cancer. She had been a flight attendant, and her family believes she was exposed to harsh chemicals through her job that eventually caused her untimely death.

In 2014, after purchasing the home, Keli and Rob invited Steve Shippy, a paranormal investigator and television personality on *Haunting in the*

Dilgert House at 919 Atchison Street, 2022. *Brooke Montoya.*

Heartland, to the home to investigate the activity they had been experiencing since remodeling it. Loving the home as she did, Keli was intent on restoring the beauty to a more original look than when the home was owned by Adam and his family. But contractors would leave before completing the work. According to an episode of the TV show, contractors heard footsteps and reported seeing shadow figures. One contractor interviewed for the show, Joey, told of how he found a blackbird in the basement with its eyes gouged out and decided his job was done there. During renovations of the

Dilgert House sign, 2022. *Brooke Montoya.*

home, Keli reported finding an old cavalry boot in the basement under the location of the original front doorway. The superstition or ritual of placing a shoe in a wall, a chimney, under a floorboard or in an attic during construction of a home has existed since the sixteenth century in the United Kingdom and as late as the 1930s in the United States. Shoes were hidden because they were thought to take on the shape of the wearer and retain the essence of the person. By hiding them, it is hoped that evil spirits will be warded off. The tradition seems especially linked to times of fear, for example during war. The cavalry boot most likely belonged to Adam, who served in the Civil War. According to the episode, the investigator believed the main floor was where the Dilgert family still resided in spirit, and they were potentially bound to the home as a result of the shoe ritual. The basement was reported to have a darker, thicker energy. Keli and Rob felt the basement was potentially a portal that needed closing. The sibling duo had a medium come and help release the Dilgert family and close the portal.

On one research trip, the home was for sale and Rob Adams allowed me and my teammate with API of Oklahoma, Tammy Christine, time in the home where we investigated each floor. Tammy Christine had a vision of a violent Adam angrily shouting as his wife ushered the children upstairs to hide when Tammy Christine first walked through the home. The basement had a heavier, more unwelcoming energy. We had the K2, a device that registers electromagnetic field fluctuations, go off several times. If it is not near anything electronic or setting off waves, it would have no reason to go off unless some anomaly touched it. To limit interference with actual electronic devices, we take baseline readings and make sure the meter goes inactivated for a time while in a location. Upstairs in the larger bedroom, we had a small ball that lights up when it is touched turn on which let us know something was present. When using our ghost box, a device that uses radio station frequencies at a quick cycling rate to allow spirit to communicate, the voice of a stern-sounding woman speaking German came through. This was likely Mrs. Dilgert. Interestingly, we also connected with Keli Adams. She said Keli

Kat, which the realtor confirmed was her nickname, and she wanted to tell her brother hello. She mentioned how ironic it was that she was now speaking to a paranormal investigator from the other side, having been a medium and investigator herself. We asked Keli if all the hauntings in Atchison are connected, and the ghost box said, "yes." This felt like confirmation of a theory I was forming while writing this book. I was since gifted a signed copy of Keli's book about Atchison by her brother Rob and hope to honor her legacy in the field and the home she so deeply loved through telling this story. The Dilgerts are buried in Mount Vernon Cemetery.

10

THEATRE ATCHISON

BEHIND THE CURTAIN

Prior to 1859, if Atchison citizens wanted entertainment, they held the events in a public hall or visited theaters in nearby cities. The first entertainment venue was built by John M. Price and was a large, three-story brick building on the corner of Fourth and Main Streets. The first floor contained storerooms, the second floor housed offices and the modern theater was on the third floor. But due to poor construction practices, the entire third floor had to be rebuilt. The Civil War abruptly stopped the theater from holding performances and became a makeshift armory. Before curtain call could happen, structural issues were found a second time, and the third floor was again rebuilt. Finally, in 1865, the first performance was held in the theater. Paddy Welsh sang patriotic songs to a sold-out crowd. John Price began adding dressing rooms, a stage and a draped curtain. Structural issues again plagued the third floor.

In 1870, construction on a large, three-story brick building, Corinthian Hall, began at North Fourth Street. The first show there was a drama called *Dora* in December of that year. This theater lasted for thirteen years until it became a roller-skating rink. The first and finest real theater was built in 1883 at the corner of Fourth Street and Kansas Avenue. This theater saw several names during its existence, including Atchison Theatre, Price's Theatre and Price's Opera House. The first show was a comedic opera, and guests filled the red plush seats. The theater operated until the end of 1893, when financial difficulties forced Price to sell the building to Captain John Seaton. Seaton remodeled the building and restored its original name,

Theatre Atchison. Due to exit law issues passed by the state legislature, renovations would be too costly, and after Seaton's death, his estate sold the building in 1912. Atchison was without a theater until Memorial Hall was built in 1922. Eventually, other halls were erected that hosted various types of theatrical entertainment.

The current Atchison Theatre is located in the building that was once Christian Science Church, erected in 1914. Christian Science followers did not believe in modern medicine, nor did they go to the doctor. They instead prayed for healing. If that did not occur, then healing was not meant to be. Many churchgoers died from illnesses. The congregation died off and sold the church to the Presbyterian congregation under the promise that they would not destroy the building and turn it into a parking lot. Most citizens still walked during this time, but driving was becoming more prevalent and the need for parking a growing concern. The Presbyterian Community Church bought the building and used it for community efforts, including variety shows and Chautauquas.

In 1984, the city found enough interest for a community theater, and Theatre Atchison was born again. The executive director, Travis Grossman, has worked at the theater for twenty years, has served on the Atchison

Theatre Atchison, 2022. *Brooke Montoya.*

Tourism Committee, including as chairman, for eight years, even winning the Tourism of the Year Award twice. He explained that the history of Atchison is rooted in haunted history because of the city's foot traffic. He worked on a documentary about Atchison's history, *Footprints*, that took nearly seven years to film and produce. By foot traffic, Travis is referring to the pioneers who emigrated from other countries or traveled from the coast to settle in the expanded West of America.

Travis happily met with me and my API teammate Tammy Christine, to give a tour and tell us the history and hauntings the theater's staff have experienced. Travis excitedly told us that the theater has a lot of energy. He explained that when guests come to the theater, they happily enjoy the show getting a break from their daily lives. Actors take on various roles that allow them to live out various lives via diverse characters. It is an escape from reality. This emotion and passion can lead to lingering souls who wish to remain connected to the ongoing activities in the building. While sitting in Travis's office, Tammy Christine asked him who the lady in the 1930s maroon Bonneville dress was. Tammy pointed up toward the stairs that ascend to the second floor. Travis laughed and said he had never seen an actual woman, but he hears footsteps on those stairs every day. He explained that it is as though a person is stepping off the stairs into the lobby area on the second floor. But the lobby is locked, so there is no possibility that a real person is walking around upstairs.

He also shared that many people hear voices, and kids who are in several performances a year have also had experiences. Travis's son would often come to programming. Once, while Travis was sitting in the front row, he turned and looked behind him and saw a headless man in the back of the theater. Travis said something to the man sitting next to him, and the man confirmed that he also saw the headless figure. Then Travis's son piped up after overhearing them and confirmed that he saw the headless man all the time. During our tour, I sat in the theater to explore this energy. I pointed to the corner where I felt the headless man had been seen, and Travis confirmed that this was where his son saw the headless man.

He also shared stories of others' experiences in the theater. A technical director was pulling an all-night shift at the venue when he heard noises in the attic, including talking, people counting pocket change and footsteps. He didn't call the police, assuming that vagrants had gone up there to sleep. He went to investigate. But no dust had been disturbed, no items had been moved and the attic was empty. Another employee, Charles

Audience seating inside Theatre Atchison, 2022. *Brooke Montoya.*

White, turned all the lights off in the theater and heard someone in the dark say, "Hey!," as if to convey that Charles had turned the lights off while someone was still working. Charles turned the lights back on but saw no one. One Halloween night, he was working late and suddenly heard the front doors of the theater start to rattle as if they were locked and someone was frantically trying to open them. Being Halloween, Charles chalked it up to kids pranking him, so he ignored it. A bit of time passed, and it happened again, so Charles quickly opened the doors. No one was there. Charles had other experiences, such as lights being turned on and off, the sound of voices and feeling that someone was there when he was working alone. Charles, a dear friend, technical director and designer, died unexpectedly of cancer. The weekend after he passed away, the theater held a show. Oddly, the lights in the men's bathroom didn't work the entire night, so staff put a lamp in the facility so that it could be used over the weekend. The following Tuesday, Travis called an electrician, who found nothing wrong with the lights after inspecting the site. The bathroom has not had an electrical issue since then. Travis explained that it was as if Charles was letting everyone know he was there and doing OK.

During my tour, I picked up on the maintenance closet, which felt full of energy. It gave off a heaviness that was very different from the rest of that area upstairs. The area includes a space that was a reading room when the building was a church. Tammy Christine and I also picked up on heavy energy in the technical section upstairs.

The theater holds four youth actor shows and four adult actor shows per year. Come enjoy the hard work put on by these dedicated actors. You might see the headless audience member sitting beside you.

11
AMELIA EARHART BIRTHPLACE MUSEUM

STILL FLYING HIGH

An Atchison treasure is undoubtedly the Amelia Earhart Birthplace Museum at 223 North Terrace Street, the home where the famous flyer was born and lived for the formative years of her childhood. Built in 1861 the wood-frame Gothic Revival cottage sits facing west overlooking the Missouri River. The world-famous Amelia Earhart, aviator and author, among other things, was a force in a patriarchal time and successfully channeled her determination to break many glass ceilings. As a child, Amelia not only collected news articles of women doing predominately male-dominated jobs but also refused to wear dresses like other girls in town. She encouraged women to reject normative social roles and set world records, including the first female to fly solo across the Atlantic Ocean. Known as one of the most influential American figures in aviation from the late 1920s through the 1930s, her life came to a mysterious end during an attempt to become the first woman to complete a circumnavigational flight of the globe in 1937. Her plane disappeared over the central Pacific Ocean. Her death is still a mystery, and there are many conspiracy theories about her disappearance, including her abduction by aliens. The museum adamantly disputes these theories.

Born in her maternal grandparents' home on July 24, 1897, Amelia was the second birth to parents Samuel "Edwin" Stanton Earhart and Amelia "Amy" Otis Earhart, her older sibling having been stillborn. Another sibling, a sister endearingly called "Pidge," was born two years later. Amelia, nicknamed "Meeley," was a firecracker from the beginning. Described as

Amelia Earhart giving her last speech in Atchison in the Memorial Building, following a parade in which the city honored the accomplished aviator, 1935. *Atchison Historic Society*.

"independent and adventurous," she preferred bloomers to dresses, which her mother supported. Meeley and Pidge loved exploring the Atchison neighborhood, hunting rats and climbing trees. In 1904, with her uncle's help, she built a ramp off the roof of the family toolshed and attempted to sled down in a wooden box. Successful but a bit battered, she exclaimed excitedly, "It was just like flying!"

Amelia's family moved to Kansas City because of her dad's employment with the railroad. Their new home was only a short trip from Atchison on the train, and Amelia visited her grandparents often and always felt it was her childhood home. Amelia's maternal grandfather was Alfred Gideon Otis, a former federal judge and prominent attorney of Otis & Glick, president of Atchison Savings Bank and leading citizen of the city. Born in New York in 1827, he moved to Atchison during its earliest years, in 1855, and he resided there until his death on May 7, 1912, in the family home. He was found dead in his bed when a servant went to let him know breakfast was ready. Charley Parks, a tenant at the home, reported hearing Otis go to the restroom around midnight. None of the family was at home during his sudden death except for his son Theodore. Mrs. Amelia Otis also died in the home in February of the same year surrounded by loved ones, neighbors and family members Mr. and Mrs. J.M. Challis. Together, Alfred and Amelia Otis had eight children, two dying in infancy. Another son, Carl S. Otis, died in the home after getting sick in 1910. He had just reached success in his career as a young adult before falling ill.

Amelia Earhart's mother, Amy Otis Earhart, grew up in Atchison and often did charitable work in the community as a teen. She and other girls in Atchison would wrap donated presents and hand them out to the less fortunate residents. She married Amelia's father, Ed Earhart of Kansas City, on October 7, 1895. When Amelia's grandmother died suddenly, she left the affluent estate and all its contents to auction because she feared Amelia's father would mishandle the Otis family fortune, as he had done with his own money in the past. Amy, Amelia's mother, was hurt and resentful that the family heirlooms went to those who purchased them at auction instead of being passed down to her. Amelia was quoted as saying that the auction was "the end of her childhood," as she had to bid farewell to the family home that was so special to her. An Atchison citizen, Dr. Eugene J. Bribach, saved the Otis family home when he donated $100,000 to Amelia Earhart's foundation, Ninety-Nines, an organization founded to educate, support and provide scholarships for women interested in aviation. It was able to purchase and restore her beloved childhood home

Amelia Earhart Birthplace Museum, 2022. *Courtesy of Hayleigh Diebolt. Locally Atchison and Visit Atchison Kansas.*

and convert it into a museum to honor the aviator. The Otis family has a large plot in Mount Vernon Cemetery.

Tammy Christine and I were able to visit the museum and investigate after it closed for the day. Using our paranormal equipment, we explored the house. The director had told us of reported activity. She mentioned that employees had seen flashes of light. A former employee, Brenda, was pushed on the stairs, and a previous caretaker who stayed overnight heard footsteps on the stairs and lights coming on by themselves. While we were there, the room with the most energetic pull was Amelia's bedroom. Energetic pull can feel different for various people, but often the air feels more alive or heavier. My legs tingle as if energy is running through them.

Amelia's childhood bedroom is suited for a little girl, including a bed, a dresser, a book she read as a child and white wallpaper adorned with yellow flowers. I felt connected to this wallpaper, because it reminded me of Afterlife Paranormal Investigations of Oklahoma's logo: a girl ghost wearing a white sheet with yellow flowers. In the room is also a dresser drawer that Amelia's grandmother made and had Amelia's named burned into as a gift for her granddaughter, dated 1904. As the house is now a museum, in front of the bed are red velvet ropes to keep visitors off the furniture. Tammy Christine, my teammate with API of Oklahoma, and I were able to investigate the home with the museum director. In Amelia's bedroom, we put a Mel Meter on the bed. This is a device that detects both temperature change and EMF frequencies in the environment. We also placed a touch-activated light ball on the floor near us, in front of the ropes. All was quiet, except for the energy we could feel around us swirling in the air. Tammy Christine described a sensation as if the spirit was flying and whizzing around the ceiling. I said, "She is still flying high!" Although we could not confirm it was Amelia, we asked if Pidge, her sister, was in the house. I got the strong sensation that Pidge, having such a close relationship with her sister, often looked after the museum and childhood home.

Amelia Earhart's childhood bedroom, where we held part of our investigation, 2022. *Brooke Montoya.*

I mentioned this out loud, and a K2 meter on the floor, which measures EMF in the environment, lit up. The director of the museum confirmed that Amelia's sister used to visit the museum when she was alive to honor her sister and check on the upkeep.

Then Tammy got a sensation that it was quiet because the spirit wasn't happy with our Mel Meter being on the bed because it was behind the ropes, which serve the purpose of alerting museum guests where they cannot go, or what they cannot touch. She described a voice saying, "Don't go past the ropes!" in a stern, protective way. I moved the meter to the floor in front of the ropes and asked, "Is that better?" The meter immediately lit up four colors to blue; it hadn't gone off at all while on the bed. We thanked the spirit and apologized for not following the museum's rules. Collectively, the energy felt like Pidge watching over the museum in spirit and making sure everyone was respecting the childhood she and her sister so loved and the memories the museum brings to life for visitors today. Other experiences of haunted activity include employees who have seen lights turn off by themselves and heard footsteps when they were the only one in the building.

The museum is self-guided and open daily except Mondays. It often offers children's programs and encourages the learning and passion of aviation in future generations.

12

SALLIE HOUSE

SINISTER SALLIE

The story is told that it was a rainy night when a frantic mother brought her six-year-old daughter to a nearby doctor's house for an emergency appendectomy, which resulted in her death. The doctor gave the little girl anesthesia but conducted the surgery too quickly, before the medicine could numb her, and the child died of shock on the doctor's table. Because the doctor was a man, the spirit of the little girl, named Sallie, hates men and targets them when they enter the home. This is the story of Sallie, the inspiration for the naming of the infamous Sallie House at 508 North Second Street. But you cannot truly understand the story of the Sallie House without also learning about the houses that stand directly north and south of 508, as the story weaves and winds with mysterious twists. Who or what really haunts this house has yet to be discovered and may have even evolved or changed over time. No records of a child named Sallie dying can be located, but that isn't the only hole to this story, which is important to examine in seeking to unravel the mystery of the legendary Sallie House.

Our story begins in 1856, when early Irish immigrant settlers Michael "M.C." and Catherine "Kate" Finney built a home at 508 North Second Street for their growing family. Their first child, James, was born that same year. The family lived in the basement during construction of the home. Michael and Kate's second child was born two years later, but Mamie died in the residence at only fifteen months old. Agnus and Charles C. were born next. Then, when Kate was pregnant with her youngest and last child in 1872, M.C. unexpectedly died in the home. Two years after that tragedy, Kate's father fell ill and came

The house at far left is 510, Charles Finney's home. The Sallie House and family home of M.C. and Kate Finney at 508 is in the middle. The home of the oldest son, James Finney, 504, is on the right, 2023. *Courtesy Stacey Price Stoneman.*

to live with her, eventually dying in the house. Two months after that, toddler Richard Edwin, the youngest Finney child, died before his second birthday. The family experienced three deaths within a few short years.

In 1879, the oldest son, James, built his own house at 504 North Second Street, directly south of his childhood home, to be close to his family. Enticed by the promise of gold in Colorado, he deeded his home to his mom and traveled west not long after its completion. His life was cut short at forty-four years when he passed away at a hospital. His funeral was held in his family home at 508. Charles C. Finney became a medical doctor and surgeon and was known for having delivered a majority of the children born in Atchison. One can locate many articles in which Dr. Finney came to help injured children after a bobsled crash on a snowy day or during an incident at school. Charles opened a medical office at 500 Commercial Street, but after medical school he remained at his childhood home until he erected his home in 1905 directly north at 510 North Second Street. This is interesting, as he would most likely have been the physician to receive a late-night knock on the door to help a dying Sallie.

Charles C. was a renowned ice skater as a youth, often dressing as a girl and calling himself "Miss Colby of Baltimore." He was considered the roller-skating champion of Atchison. With luck on his side, he narrowly escaped death from bullets on two occasions. Once, when Charles was a boy, hunting with two men, a gun accidentally discharged, and the bullet passed between his body and right arm. In a second harrowing event, a man shot at a rabbit, and two bullets went straight through Finney's hat.

Members of Afterlife Paranormal Investigations of Oklahoma in front of the Sallie House prior to our first overnight investigations, 2021. *Standing, left to right*: Jessica Daws, Brooke Montoya and Tammy Christine. *Seated, left to right*: Jill Stokes and Amy Padgett. *Brooke Montoya*.

Charles C. married Louise Zibold, daughter of Herman and Rosa Zibold of the Zibold-Haegelin Brewery, in a surprise wedding the couple hid from both their families. They had one son, Charles H. Finney, who followed in his father's footsteps and became Dr. Charles H. Finney in 1931. Charles C. and his family never resided in 508 but spent their entire marriage in a red cottage home at 510. Charles retired from his medical practice and became the Atchison mayor in 1913. Two years into his mayoral duties, he was arrested for contempt for not enforcing the prohibition laws of the city. Charles J. Conlon, the brother-in-law of John McInteer, who resided at the McInteer Villa with his sister Anne, was Charles Finney's attorney in the case. A year later, Charles Finney was forced to resign as mayor. There are documented accounts of Charles Finney taking in boarders while his family lived at the residence at 510.

Agnus Finney lived in her childhood home at 508 for most of her life. In 1913, she married William "Bill" True. William had been married previously to a woman named Laura C. True, and together they had three children. In 1901, William and Laura lived at 617 North Second Street, just north of the Sallie House across Laramie Street, which is likely how Agnus and William met. Laura filed for divorce from William, claiming he had a "jealous disposition" and was abusive. Their case went to trial, and Laura was granted the divorce on grounds of abandonment. When Bill and Agnus married, they moved to Nebraska for his job. His youngest daughter with Laura, Ilva True, though she typically lived with her dad and Agnus, went to school in Atchison and spent summers staying with Charles C. Finney at 510. Ilva was the same age as several other girls in town, and she often had them over or attended their parties. Among these girls were Sally Snowden and Sally Ingalls. Both girls were daughters of prominent families in town. Considering their friendly connection with Ilva, I thought it interesting to pursue their ties to the house. But they were teens when attending parties with Ilva, and both moved away from Atchison and lived long lives. These are the only names I could find of girls in Atchison named Sallie or Sally. But the death of the girl in the original story might have gone undocumented.

In May 1918, Bill had a stroke while away at his and Agnus's Wyoming ranch vacation home, so the couple returned to 508 to tend to his health. Tragically, he died in the Finney home shortly after returning. A month after that, Kate Finney, the matriarch of the family, passed away at the 510 home of her son Charles. Kate had fallen down the stairs, injuring her foot. She developed gangrene and sepsis and died peacefully with her beloved Charles C. and daughter Agnus by her side. Agnus lived the remainder of her life at 508, passing away of old age in 1939. Her death was the sixth in the home. Except for the short five years she was married to Bill, Agnus lived in her childhood home all her life. She was known to take in boarders, but after she died, Charles H., the son of Charles C., lived in the home briefly. After Charles H. moved out, incidents in the home began to take on a life of their own.

Richard "Dick" Mize moved his wife and daughter Sarah "Sallie" Margaret Mize into the house at 508. This is interesting, as Sarah was a young girl with the nickname Sallie, but any connection with the girl in the story unravels because Sarah "Sallie" Margaret lived in the home for only ten years, grew up and married and then lived out her adult life in Connecticut, where she died of old age. It is also interesting to note that Richard Mize was a descendant of the Mize family that lived at the RavenHearse Mansion at Fifth and Parallel Street. For the next thirty years, a woman named Ethel Anderson owned the home at 508. According to her grandson Sterling, an employee at the Atchison Historical Society, his grandma did not report experiencing any activity during her time in the home. He recalled playing in the house and discredited scratches supposedly made by spirits as having been done by him and his brothers. From 1990 to 1992, the Humbard family moved from the house at 504 to the house at 508, and their daughter Heather told her parents that she had an imaginary friend named Sallie. This this the first documentation we have of haunted activity and the name of Sallie.

The story of the Sallie House takes a wild turn in 1992, when Tony and Deborah Pickman moved into the home while Deborah was pregnant with their first son, Taylor. Within a month of moving in, they reported lights flickering, the family dog barking at the nursery door and appliances being turned off and on by themselves. Deborah also reported that the nursery lights would turn on and remain on all night while Taylor slept in the bedroom with Deborah and Tony, and the crib mobile would play music and turn on its own. Unusual activity escalated in the home when, in July 1993, stuffed animals in the nursery were placed in a circle in the middle of the room when no one was home. Tony became more affected in an aggressive way by the activity in the house. He was scratched, and his mood became angrier. Barbara Conner, a psychic who was referred to the Pickmans by a friend, came to the home to help the family. She picked up on a little girl spirit who wanted to be called "Sallie" and suggested that the family buy the spirit a baby doll as a gift. On Halloween of the same year, Tony saw "Sallie" in his kitchen. He drew a picture, which shows a little girl in a blue dress with dark curls and matching bows in her hair. As Tony's state of mind worsened, he began to have thoughts of harming his wife by pushing her down the stairs. The couple called Ed and Lorraine Warren, nationally known for helping people with paranormal activity in their home. They didn't investigate the home, but based on what Tony shared with them, Lorraine urged him to move out of the home. She felt he and his family were in danger.

The television show *Sightings* came out to interview Tony as word spread about the home's paranormal activity. Psychic Peter James was brought in. When Tony was being interviewed, the camera crew witnessed him being scratched on his stomach in front of them. The scratches were caught on camera. This was before the influx of paranormal television shows and was groundbreaking for the time. Having had enough, Tony and Deborah moved out of the home in 1994. By now, word had spread, and everyone was interested in the house with potential demonic activity. This may have attracted some renters with darker intentions. According to Deborah Pickman's book *The Sallie House Haunting: A True Story*, the landlord found pentagrams on the basement floor and dark-magic paraphernalia after the next two renters moved out, one in 1995 and the other in 2002. Shortly after that, the City of Atchison purchased the home. Today, those brave enough can stay the night in the house to see what they experience for themselves.

One theory is that Sallie was a daughter of Dr. Finney and one of his enslaved persons. In a television special, it is depicted that he tries to hide the illegitimate child in a closet and eventually kills her. But no documentation mentions that he had servants, let alone enslaved servants, and both homes, 510 and 508, are moderately sized compared to homes in Atchison that typically employed servants. There are reports that Kate Finney cared for her own home and was very picky about her housekeeping, so it seems unlikely she would have servants. The theory of Sallie being killed by the doctor, whether this doctor was her father or when conducting a medical procedure, is still perpetuated. Many say that this is why the spirit in the house seems to attack men more than women.

Another theory is that Sallie is the ghost of Sallie Isabelle Hall, a Black woman who lived directly behind the 508 home in the late 1800s. Sallie died at thirty-three in 1905 from disease. This theory is a stretch, because the little girl Tony Pickman claims to have seen was a white girl about six years old. Unfortunately, when you look up Sallie on Find A Grave on the web, someone has linked the drawing Tony drew of Sallie to Sallie Hall as factual information. Yet another Sallie theory involves Dick Mize's daughter, nicknamed Sallie, who actually lived in the home. But she lived to adulthood in a different state.

Members of
Afterlife Paranormal
Investigations of
Oklahoma with Tony
Pickman, 2021.
Brooke Montoya.

So, who or what is Sallie? Interestingly, the first mention of activity is the Humbard family's daughter playing with an imaginary friend, according to reports. It is also interesting that when clearing North Second Street for laying the road and building houses, the city found bones of the Native American Kansa tribe. Some people think the land may be cursed; others surmise that the spirit may have been conjured. What Tony seemed to have experienced sounds like demonic oppression approaching the level of possession. Some think the demonic entity still lurks in the house at 508. Others think that, over time, investigations may have grown an egregore, a spirit created out of the thoughts of collective groups. This means that, over time, as people enter the home and try to speak with a little girl named "Sallie," the energy gets stronger and becomes that in which people focus.

Currently, the house's first floor includes the kitchen, dining room and living room, with stairs leading to the second floor. Upstairs includes three bedrooms and a bathroom. The house is small, considering that the Finney family was well-known in the town's social circles. When you enter the house, you notice that it is clean and decor is sparse, but the hunter-green carpet downstairs and mauve carpet upstairs feel frozen in time, as if Tony Pickman and family had just moved out. Having been on two overnight visits in the home with API of Oklahoma, I am still not certain what is in the home. On our first visit, in 2021, we experienced the most negative energy in the closet of the primary bedroom and had the most activity with equipment in the bedroom that was Taylor Pickman's nursery. We were able to meet with and interview Tony, and he gifted us a drawing he created to take to the home to use as a trigger object. A trigger object is an item that might induce activity, because it is of the same period as the location, is relevant to the haunted story or, in this case, was drawn by someone who was violently sought out and oppressed by a spirit in the house.

The house has a presence that feels ominous. Among our equipment is an SLS camera. The SLS uses Kinect Sensor Xbox 360 graphing software, which detects human shapes. The sensor is sensitive, and it is important to make sure it is not mapping inanimate objects in a room. The software mapped out a spirit sitting on the twin bed in the child's bedroom. We had a touch light there, so we asked the spirit to touch the light in front of it and change the light's color. On the SLS, we saw the hand move toward the touch light, then the light changed colors as if it had been touched. We then requested the spirit move across the room to the wooden rocking horse and sit on it. As we moved our SLS over, the spirit appeared on the horse. We asked the spirit to put its hand in the air, and we demonstrated as though riding a horse and waving a rope in the air. The SLS view showed the spirit moving its hand in the air.

On our second visit, we got no activity in the child's bedroom. We did hear knocks from the closed basement door. We also got interaction through our SB7 spirit box, a radio that uses AM/FM frequencies and shuffles through them at a high speed to allow spirits to come through the device and communicate. It felt like we were talking to Dick Mize based on questions being answered. Although the house has a dark feel, especially at night, we did not experience activity that is still oppressive, as some have reported. In 2022, psychic Sam Baltrusis, author Richard Estep (writer of the foreword of this book) and psychic medium Jessica Potter took a tour of the home. Sam felt an immediate sickness take over him, as though he was being manipulated. Jessica picked up on the energy of what was happening inside the house as she waited outside, each of them taking a turn going in alone. She confirmed Sam's sense that it

Drawing of Jesus
with a crown of
thorns by Tony
Pickman, 2021.
Brooke Montoya.

felt like an attack. She did not have the same experience, potentially confirming the idea of how differently the entity treats men and women.

The Sallie House is one of the most popular locations for visitors to Atchison. Even local college students report crossing the street instead of walking on the sidewalk near the house. The house has been featured on paranormal shows like *Sightings* (1990s), *Ghost Adventures* (2015), twice on *BuzzFeed Unsolved* (2021), *A Haunting* (2006) and in the full-length documentary *The Sallie House: The Most Haunted House in America* (2009), *Most Haunted Town, Unexplained Mysteries* and *My Ghost Story*. If you think you are brave enough to find out what is haunting the Sallie House, you can rent it for an overnight stay or do a one-hour self-guided tour. The Finney family members are buried in Mount Calvary Cemetery.

13

GLICK MANSION

GHOSTLY GOVERNOR'S WIFE

For many years, when coming to Atchison, visitors could enjoy the history and hauntings of the Glick Mansion at the Tuck U Inn Bed and Breakfast. The owners of the mansion at 503 North Second Street, across from the infamous Sallie House, loved and cared for the home, allowing the history to live on. The inn was featured as one of the "Most Haunted Hotels of Kansas." Unfortunately, in 2021, the property was sold, so the Glick Mansion's future is uncertain. The spirits of the house might be unsettled as they wait to see who will care for the home they refuse to leave.

George W. Glick's life is one of remarkable achievements and great tragedies. The family's energetic imprint on the mansion is indisputable, as generations lived in the home for seventy-one years. Built in 1873 and placed on the National Register of Historic Places in 1992, the Glick-Orr House was originally High Victorian Gothic in style. George purchased two lots for his home for $950. The house was under continuous construction, which lasted for thirty-nine years. In 1879, Glick's wife, Lizzie, purchased two adjoining lots just north of the home for $1,000, and the mansion was expanded. In 1913, two years after George Glick's death, the house was left to his daughter Jennie and her husband, James W. Orr. They remodeled the property, redesigning the style to reflect Tudor Revival. The house is called the Glick-Orr Mansion, because James Orr created his own notoriety in the city, serving in the Kansas House of Representatives and living in the home most of his adult life after marrying Jennie.

Born on a farm in Ohio, George Glick continued the farming lifestyle, owning Shannon Hill Farm in Atchison. The Glick farm comprised 640 acres and is one of the most famous in the state. Even after beginning his career as a lawyer, he helped his father farm in Ohio and was known for saying his father was the best farmer he ever knew. His grandfather emigrated from Germany and was a soldier in the War of 1812. George's father most likely inspired his desire to be in politics, as Isaac Glick was not only a farmer but also treasurer of Sandusky County, Ohio, for three terms. George was highly educated. The first school he attended was the "Glick Schoolhouse," at which he later taught at the age of nineteen. He then attended a school founded by Dr. Dio Lewis, the famous temperance leader, preacher, feminist and social reformer. A career as a lawyer might not have always been in George's plan, but while working on the farm, he caught his foot in a threshing machine. He fully recovered and, shortly after coming to Atchison, opened a law partnership, Glick & Otis, with Amelia Earhart's grandfather, prominent Atchison judge Alfred G. Otis. George also helped organize Washington Lodge No. 5 in Atchison and was a member of all three local Masonic bodies at the time of his death.

George married Elizabeth Ryder Glick, and together they had two children, Frank, who moved to Kansas City, and Jennie. Jennie lived in the Glick-Orr Mansion after marrying her husband and raised their son George Glick Orr in the home. George Glick was the ninth, and only Democratic, governor to that time when his death was reported in 1911. A statue of him stood in Statuary Hall in the U.S. Capitol Building in Washington. Each state selects two prominent citizens to be recognized for literature, art, the military or civic life. The statue remained there until 2003, when it was being replaced with a statue of Dwight D. Eisenhower. George's wife, "Lizzie," had a prominent and distinguished colonial ancestry. She was known for her poise and grace and set a new standard for the state's first ladies. During this phase of his career, George developed a throat infection that destroyed his ability to speak, forcing him to end his career in politics.

It would be expected that retirement from a successful career would be a joyous time of rest and enjoyment, but George's throat issue was just one of many tragedies to happen in a domino effect leading to his death. The first traumatic experience occurred in January 1909, when George attended a political conference at the famous and first hotel in Kansas, the Copeland Hotel in Topeka. In the middle of the night, the hotel caught fire; within an hour, only its walls remained. Ex-governor Glick was carried down the ladder from the third-floor fire escape without injury. He had to be carried

Glick Mansion, located at 503 North Second Street, 2022. *Brooke Montoya.*

due to his age and an injury. He had fallen on the ice that winter, hurting his hip. The summer of the same year, George's grandson and Jennie Orr's only son, George Glick Orr, got married. The couple took a honeymoon trip to La Jolla Beach in San Diego, California. He was twenty-five, studied law like his father and grandfather and had purchased a home that was filled with wedding gifts waiting the couple's return. While lying on the beach with his new wife, George joked about how he planned to lie there until the tide carried him away. In a twist of fate, a large wave came over him and carried him out to sea. His wife could only watch in horror. His body never resurfaced and was never recovered. He had been raised with his parents in his grandparents' home, and this loss was profound for George Glick and Jennie Orr, losing their only child and grandchild.

George Glick had a winter home with an orange grove in Florida. It was here in 1910 that he fell for a second time and broke his hip. He returned to Atchison to heal but died a year later at eighty-three in the Glick-Orr Mansion. His wife, one of the founders and a charter member of the Atchison Public Library for twenty-five years, died and had her funeral in the home in 1919. Jennie and James Orr continued to live in and remodel the home until James died in 1927. Jennie remained until her death in 1944. The Glick-Orr family has a large plot in Mount Vernon Cemetery.

With no surviving children left, the home was divided up among the family's church, relatives and the Atchison Public Library. The estate sold the mansion to mortician William Stanton Jr. in 1945 for $4,000. He resided there until 1962, and after his death, his wife sold the property to James M. and Christeen Griffith. There were two other owners after the Griffiths until Ray and Joyce Barmby of the Tuck U Inn purchased the property in 1992.

The bed-and-breakfast embraced the historical and haunted occurrences. Many who stayed at the hotel reported sounds of footsteps and doors being opened and closed when nobody was touching them. According to the website Boiseghost.org, Angela Jane claims that people have reported seeing full-body apparitions of what is believed to be George and Lizzie watching over their home, roaming quietly from room to room. A family member of Angela Jane's described how a chair suddenly showed an indention in the foam, as if something unseen had sat down.

Our team, API of Oklahoma, drove up to the Glick Mansion and parked in front, allowing Tammy Christine to connect to the energy of the home, as we could not go inside. Our approach was to drive Tammy Christine around while she was blindfolded and stop at various locations to see what she could pick up with her psychic skills. Additionally, we used various pieces of investigation equipment. Immediately, Tammy Christine connected with a female not in the best of health. Tammy Christine described the female spirit as sad and wandering around the home, looking for the previous owner, whom she used to follow around. This spirit missed the fresh flowers the owner brought into the home and wanted her to come back. The lady spirit felt it was too quiet. On the ghost word generator, we got *smell*. Then Tammy began to describe an incident that happened at the corner of Second and Parallel Streets. She described seeing horses and a buggy with a child inside looking out. A man was in the road and was trampled by the horses. Tammy described seeing the images from the man's perspective and the man seeing the little girl in the buggy react to his death. Tammy felt that the man hangs out in the kitchen area of the home. Unfortunately, in spirit, he relives his death daily. We then got the words *pick* and *drive*. In my research I could not locate a news article that told of this story, although not all deaths were reported. However, the lady that Tammy picked up on that wanders the house is interesting since Ray and Joyce Barmby recently sold the property after having owned it for some time. It makes sense the spirits of the house feel it is too quiet after it was a bustling bed-and-breakfast and the owners cared for the home for so many years. Hopefully, new residents will embrace the ghosts who roam the Glick Mansion and bring them fresh flowers occasionally.

14

NELLIE TRUEBLOOD

LESSONS IN THE AFTERLIFE

C aptain Alva C. Trueblood and his wife, Harriet, lived in the home at 526 North Third Street their entire lives. Together they had six children, including Nellie, Victor and Narval, the latter dying in the home as an infant. Harriet had many friends, but Nellie was her closest companion. Harriet Eliza Allen Trueblood was born in Salem, Indiana, where she also met and married A.C. They came to Atchison in 1881 and were well-known in the community. A.C. was captain of Company A, Thirteenth Indiana Infantry Regiment during the Civil War (1861–65), participating in many of the most "hotly contested battles of war," according to his obituary. Residents of Atchison often reported that he gave vivid accounts of the human lives lost during his time in battle and "told of how a person could walk for miles on the dead bodies with which the field was strewn." When he came to Atchison, he was first a farmer, then a merchant. He served as city clerk from 1885 to 1904 and was also successful in the insurance business. A newspaper article from 1899 reports a family reunion at the home, the first one held in ten years, as various family members had planted roots all over the United States. A.C. passed away in April 1904 in the residence. For twenty years after his passing, Harriet and Nellie lived at North Third Street, until Harriet died in the home at eighty-four with Nellie and Victor at her bedside.

Nellie was a beloved teacher at Ingalls School and, according to the *Atchison Daily Globe*, had a major interest in educating the underprivileged and was active in missionary work as a reporter and a regent for Daughters of the American Revolution. Nellie never married. She resided with a woman named Helen McKendrick, who also never married. A newspaper article reported that Helen was Nellie's housekeeper and companion and that the two lived together for twenty-five years. Helen died in 1948 at eighty-two in a tragic car accident. Helen and Nellie had spent the day at Mr. and Mrs. Ernest H. Sward's home, and the Swards were taking the two back to their home on Third Street when the Swards' 1941 Chevrolet Coach collided with a 1940 Ford Coupe driven by Edward White, twenty-one. White's car struck the passenger side of the Sward vehicle, hitting Mrs. Sward, who was in the right-side back seat, and Helen, in the front passenger seat. Nellie, sitting in the seat behind Ernest who was driving, was uninjured, as was Mr. Sward. Helen died thirty minutes after the accident due to a fractured skull, and Mrs. Sward suffered severe internal injuries. After Helen's death, Nellie Trueblood lived alone in the home until her passing ten years later, on April 24, 1958. Although Nellie died in the hospital, according to her nephew she lived in the home her entire life. Members of the Daughters of the American Revolution held a graveside service for her at Mount Vernon Cemetery.

According to the book of collected oral stories published by the chamber of commerce, recent homeowners Don and Martha reported unexplainable and shocking activity. While remodeling the home, they might have seen the spirit of Nellie in the form of a brightly colored orb eighteen to twenty-four inches in size. On another occasion, Martha thought she saw the furnace on fire and frantically called the fire department. On inspection, the furnace had no burns, nothing was charred and there was no smoke. According to an article on the website Legends of America, Nellie's nephew Scott

Nellie Trueblood House located at 526 North Third Street, 2022. *Brooke Montoya.*

Neilson said that he would not be surprised if the orb of light that people report seeing was Nellie's ghost. Scott said, "There was a lot of love in that old home." The home is currently being rented, and according to the most recent renters, who have resided there for a year, there have been no unusual occurrences. Maybe Nellie has moved on, or perhaps she has learned to share the love of her home with the earth-bound humans. Having lived in the home for seventy-seven years, it is understandable that she would choose to stay and watch over the special residence that held her life's memories. This house has been a popular spot on the city's haunted trolley tour in past years.

15

ELKS LODGE

LONGING TO BE HEARD

The Atchison branch of the Elks Lodge, No. 647, located now at 609 Kansas Avenue, was founded in 1901. The Elks is a social club that began in 1868 in New York City, when actors and entertainers of the city did not want to follow liquor regulations. They wanted to be able to drink on Sundays without paying extra taxes and originally called themselves the "Jolly Corks." The club evolved into a proper fraternal order with an emphasis on benevolence and charity. The elk was chosen to represent the fraternal order because it is a distinctly American animal. The Atchison club still exists and serves local youth, veterans and others in need through volunteering, fundraising and programs.

In 2018, the Elks Lodge celebrated its 150th anniversary with Ron Keller as the Exalted Ruler. Some honored members have held membership for over sixty years. The club sponsors sporting competitions, drug awareness programs and scholarships, and every year it adopts twenty-five to thirty local families in need for Christmas. When the fraternal order was established in Atchison, many notable citizens were part of the lodge. J.M. Challis was the Toastmaster and John M. Price the Exalted Ruler. At a meeting in 1917, more than one hundred members were present during roll call. A news article stated the club had to begin holding members-only dances as a way to attract younger men to join. Another article mentioned the importance of the Elks in the men's lives. One man, W. Glenneby, a former employee of Blish, Mize, & Silliman, enlisted in the U.S. Marines. He wrote a letter to lodge members back home while he was deployed about his experiences. He wrote that three other Elk members were in his platoon, from Chicago and New York. This shows the camaraderie and connection these men had as a result of belonging to this organization.

While at the post office with my team API of Oklahoma, we investigated outside in the parking lot. Tammy Christine was blindfolded so that she had no information as to where we were in town. Jill Stokes informed me of words being generated by the ghost word generator. The thing about spirits is that you never know who wants to be heard and why. In the current situation, even though we were at the post office, a different spirit longed to be heard and connected with us. Tammy Christine immediately began picking up on a male. She said that he was showing her that he was having trouble breathing. She also saw women at a social gathering. We were in front of the post office, so I thought to myself, "How does this fit?" Tammy Christine proceeded to say that there was a monument outside with signage. She also said she saw a flagpole. I looked next door and, in my amazement, got Jill's attention and pointed quietly at the Elks Lodge. I was putting together that Tammy Christine was picking up on that location instead, but did not want to help her with any information. Outside were both the monument of the Elk and the flagpole. Tammy Christine explained that the women heard the muzzle of a gun and were startled. She described seeing their faces; they were in shock and scared. Finally, she described a fence-like part of the building. This was likely the second-floor wood decor that adorns the Elks building. With all of these details, I felt that Tammy was actually picking up on the ghosts connected to the Elks Lodge rather than the post office. I made notes and revealed to her where we were and what I thought was interesting about her connections to the Elks Lodge. When we returned to the location where we were staying in town, I dove into research. I wanted to know about the Elks Lodge and its history. In minutes, I happened upon an article about Edward O. Bradley.

Edward O. Bradley was a retired farmer and a member of the Elks Lodge responsible for distributing charity funds. He was described as conscientious and careful and a capable bookkeeper. But in March 1913, Bradley went into the lodge's secretary's office and wrote a note: "I have violated a moral obligation. See Charles A. Brown." Bradley and Brown were set to meet at 1:00 p.m. that day to audit some of the Elks' charity bills. Instead, Bradley took his life, shooting himself in the right temple with a revolver at noon. Others were in the building and heard the gunshot. They ran to Bradley's aid, but he had already perished. Bradley had many difficulties in his life, including his potential future son-in-law, George Mueller. George had been

Elks Lodge, 2023. *Brooke Montoya.*

dating Bradley's daughter Olive, but Bradley told his daughter that she had to choose between him and George. It was rumored that Bradley even threatened George's life. Bradley had been vocal about his desire to end his life with friends and family, but they did not take it seriously. He even called Jake Hastings, steward at the Elks lodge, and told him what he planned to do. Bradley left behind a wife and two children, Olive, twenty, and Robert, seventeen. Edward is buried at Mount Vernon Cemetery.

This story was almost exactly what Tammy Christine had picked up on outside the post office. I wonder if Bradley had regrets he wanted to make others aware of or even if in spirit he was trying to be heard, as nobody in his life took his threats and pleas seriously. I wonder what else Bradley would like to share with us about his life and his story if given the opportunity. If you are at the Elks lodge, take the opportunity to say "hello" to Bradley. Maybe he will say "hello" back. He definitely is longing to be heard.

16

RAVENHEARSE MANOR

FRIGHT AT FIRST BITE

Colonel William Osborne, a man of wealth, loved his daughter so much that he built her a home in 1884. She was marrying Mr. Parks, a notable Atchison bachelor, and they would start their life in the manor. William Osborne was a railway baron from the East who came to Atchison to build the Central Branch of the Union Pacific Railroad. The colonel spared no expense in building the home, at a total cost of $26,462.60. The house stands on a quarter of a block off-center, which creates a large west yard. In 1894, "the most interesting drama in the social life of Atchison" occurred. The party of all parties was being planned, but amid the arrangements, a smallpox outbreak occurred, and city residents were forced to shelter in place. No gatherings were permitted. Two days before the quarantine expired, the Kansas Board of Health was contacted, and since no new cases had appeared for ten days, Mr. Park's party was allowed to be held. Over three hundred invitations went out to Atchison residents. Unfortunately, two days later, the day before the party, police discovered new cases in a residence in North Atchison and extended the quarantine.

This was unacceptable to Mr. Parks since he had already spent a considerable amount of money to prepare for the party and was adamant it not go to waste. He decided to move forward with the party despite the extended quarantine. Rumors began circulating about the police interfering with the party, so Parks hired an attorney. Judge Webb explained that the only way to stop the police was to file an injunction. Parks did, and a trial was set for the morning of the party. The judge surprised everyone and denied

RavenHearse House, located at 517 Parallel Street, 2023. *Bill RavenHearse.*

the injunction. It was hours before the party was to begin, and musicians were only fifteen minutes from arriving to prepare. The only way to send a notice to invited guests of cancelation was the newspaper; partygoers could not be notified quickly enough. Police officers set up barricades at locations around the house, and many people were denied entry. Some guests got creative and hopped the fence and entered through the back of the home. The news reported that a girl was kicked by a cow and a boy split his trousers trying to gain entry to the party. Around 8:30 p.m., the pianist began playing a waltz, and guests began dancing on the constructed dance floor outside. Quickly, police officers came to the door. The dancing and the arrival of police continued, to the amusement of partygoers. Those outside who had not yet gained entrance cheered every time dancing resumed. Most all had succeeded in gaining entry to the party by midnight, and overall the police were polite and courteous. The guests even shared ice cream with the police.

In a written history of the Mize family by William R. Mize, he tells of his parents buying the home in 1918 while his mother was pregnant. Mr. and Mrs. Mize had a total of seven children, of whom five survived. One of his siblings died after a fall that cut his lip. He developed blood poisoning and died at two and a half years old. His sister Virginia died during the peak of the Spanish flu epidemic. His entire family contracted the disease, and Edna Bonnell, a nurse, came to stay in the home to care for the family. Virginia was the only family member to die of the flu, at three and a half years old. William Mize is unsure if it is true or a lie his siblings made up to scare him, but he was always told that a previous resident of the home buried a baby on the property.

William described the neighbors next door having a "house [that] contributed an aura of evil and mystery" when he was younger. The man was frightening and the woman "sour." There was speculation that, one day, the only dog the family ever owned was poisoned by the scary neighbors. It was found dead by their barn. The Mize family has a spacious plot located at Mount Vernon Cemetery.

The home's floors and railings are all made from maple wood, and the doors still have skeleton keys. I was lucky enough to get a private tour from current owner Bill RavenHearse. The house has a billiards room. Bill explained that this is where the men gathered. On moving in, Bill and his family found a secret passageway from the billiards room to the bathroom. Across from it was the parlor. Entering this room, I felt an electric energy. I mentioned this heavy energy to Bill, and he explained this room was the location where at least six family members passed away and where their wakes were held. He explained that once someone got too ill, it was difficult for them to be upstairs, so their bed would be moved downstairs into this large room with a fireplace. They would be cared for. At their death, the room served as the traditional parlor room for wakes, a common practice at that time. Bill and his family are in the process of restoring the home, although it is unlikely to be approved for the National Register of Historic Places, as there are no original pictures of the home's interior. An interesting feature of the home is the stained-glass window on the stairs. When it was installed, it was not aligned properly. The window is three separate stained-glass pieces that are supposed to form one image, but the window slats were installed in the wrong order. This was left as a mistake and serves as a unique talking piece. The kitchen is on the first floor and has the original sink, as well as a large space that looks like a pantry but was an original icebox.

Also on the first floor is a beautiful, narrow dining room that boasts rare and pricey wallpaper. When we entered this room, an electric candlestick came on by itself. While interviewing Bill about the home, I was honored to sit at the head of the table in a large, prominent chair. Bill and his family hold what they call "Interview with a Vampire" events at Halloween. He begins the evening dressed in his theater-quality costume, which takes over three hours to put on, and welcomes guests into his lair. He serves red punch. While sitting in the dining room, Bill shared with us heartwarming stories of his children and spoke of the recent loss of his son Rocky. I could feel energy circling around us while he beamed with pride, telling us of how Rocky loved to play pranks on guests, catching them off-guard to get the best jump scares. Rocky was honored by the community and his family after his passing with a funeral in the front yard near what remained of the famous oak tree. On December 2, 1859, Abraham Lincoln came to Atchison and gave a practice speech by that same oak tree, which is memorialized on a plaque near the Atchison County Courthouse. Now only the stump remains. Rocky's untimely passing saved nine lives: his brothers, who now know of the genetic heart condition; and five persons who received organ donations.

Bill recounted how the house found him while taking the haunted trolley tour sixteen years ago. He explained that he visited once a year to see family nearby, and in 2019, he noticed the house was for sale. He and his family were living in Arizona at the time and were so drawn to the home that they sold their house in Tucson. He said he knew he was experiencing a synchronicity, because his house in Arizona had a similar interior decor as a casket with a pink rose he saw when viewing the house. The details were too similar to ignore, and the house already felt like his. Bill explained that, one day, a couple in their eighties showed up, asking to see the home. They said that they had lived there once. The man told Bill that when he was a child, they were not allowed in the dining room, because it was the "fancy room" and that they always hated the basement.

The second floor is mostly bedrooms, all with gorgeous and unique fireplaces. The attic is an interesting space that Bill called the "pandemic room." An interesting signature is in the attic, "Dia," dated 1918. In my review of family names, I found that the Mize family lived here during the flu epidemic. This was also reported in William Mize's writings of his family history. The name Dia cannot be located among the known family of that time, but could likely be a nickname. The attic is where Bill keeps Halloween decor, themed costumes and other items for their events. He pointed out a large mannequin that was once placed in the attic window. Its head was found to have been turned when nobody had been in the attic. Bill explained that this is where a lot of activity happens in the home. The basement is similar to other homes in Atchison and spans the entire property, with sectioned-off rooms. Bill houses thirteen real coffins he has collected over the years. The best part of the tour, besides meeting the warm and welcoming

Me and Marius, the raven pet and family member at RavenHearse, after building trust, 2021. *Brooke Montoya.*

Bill and seeing this beautiful treasure of a house, was meeting Marius Raven, a black raven that is truly a member of the family. He has full flight of the home and sleeps on a dog bed in Bill's room. Bill has had Marius for nine years. The raven will likely live to approximately fifty years old. Bill has permits and licenses to have him as a pet, and Marius knows hundreds of words and commands. We got to build trust with Marius, to the point that he sat on our arms. He even has his own Facebook page.

Bill says the house is very active but that the ghosts are friendly and respectful. During tours, guests note the smell of baby powder and report feeling a tug on the back of their shirt. The family has seen a little girl running up and down the

RavenHearse dining room, the "pretty room" the children were not allowed in and the beginning location for the "Interview with a Vampire" event, 2022. *Brooke Montoya.*

stairs. She also likes to remove knobs on a dresser. Anything electronic in the home is privy to be turned off and on by itself. You can join Bill for one of his "Interview with a Vampire" events during the spooky season of Halloween and get an inside look at this beautiful home. Make sure to drink the blood, and watch out for any tricksters. You never know who is waiting to catch you off-guard for a good laugh.

17

CRAY HISTORICAL HOME MUSEUM

SUPERVISING SPIRIT

This house at 805 North Fifth Street steals your breath as you take in the beauty. It is the epitome of Victorian-era wealth. The enormous white mansion dominates the block of Fifth Street. It was built in 1882 by W.W. Hetherington, son of the founder of Exchange National Bank of Atchison, at a cost of between $6,500 and $8,500. On a trip to Europe, Mrs. Hetherington fell in love with the towers of Scotland castle architecture. So, when the couple returned home, they tore off a corner of the house and installed a three-story tower at a cost of $10,000, more than the cost of the original house. With a total of twenty-five rooms and five fireplaces, the home was added to the National Register of Historic Places in 1974. Eye-catching features are the tower and the unique carriage entry. The entry is a large covered patio where carriages would pull up and guests would enter the home.

Webster Wert Hetherington was known around town as the "Atchison Millionaire" and the "Duke of Kansas." Born in 1850 in Pennsylvania, he came to Atchison in 1859 with his parents, Mr. and Mrs. William Hetherington. His father established Exchange National Bank. When Webster grew up, he followed in the family business. In 1875, he married Lillie Miller, and together they had five children: Webster Wert, Gail, Harry, Mary Louise and Ruthanna. A cunning businessman, he succeeded his father as president of the bank after his father's death. Mr. Hetherington died at forty-two years old in 1892, only ten years after the home was built. Since his brother was not old enough to take over his position in the bank, Mr.

Hetherington House at 805 North Fifth Street, date unknown. *Courtesy Atchison Historical Society.*

Balie Peyton Waggener was appointed president. The newspaper reported that Mr. Hetherington's house and yard were filled with friends and residents of the community for his funeral service. The streets were lined for two blocks with carriages, and the procession was the largest ever seen in the city, covering five blocks. He was clearly a beloved resident.

A special family tradition at Christmas Eve was to light a candle in each window. Mrs. Hetherington lived in the home until she passed away in 1937. Son Wert Hetherington joined the banking business as a cashier. He became blind in his later years and passed away in the home. While the Hetheringtons owned the home, they hosted others' funerals in the parlor. One of the funerals was for Bill Adams, a friend of the family. Sallie Snowden, a little girl of a prominent Atchison family, really took to Bill and wanted him to attend her sixth birthday party. Her party was held at the lake, and while swimming, Bill dove into the water and never surfaced. Sallie tried to help the grown man up but could not. Her dad noticed what was happening and pulled Bill to the shore. They revived him, but after three days in the hospital, Bill died from his injuries. Bill's funeral and wake were

Cray Historical Home Museum, 2022. *Brooke Montoya.*

held in the Hetherington home. Fredrick "Fred" Stein, the inventor of the first electric radio, died in the home. He and his wife had fallen ill and took up residence there. Fred died in the Cray home in 1972. One of his radios is on display in the guest parlor room.

The Hetheringtons lived in the home consecutively for eighty years. In 1962, it was purchased by Steve Stanton, vice-president of Exchange National Bank, and the family lived there for six years. The Stantons honored the Hetheringtons by carrying on the tradition of lighting candles in each window on Christmas Eve. The Stantons had two children, Sheila and Richard. Sheila's wedding reception was hosted in the home, but tragedy hit the family when Richard passed away of encephalitis at twenty-four years old. It was next purchased by Dr. Richard Sames, the first lay dean of St. Benedict's College. Dr. Sames lived in the home for four years. After this, it stood abandoned and was mistreated by vandals. In 1973, Harry Peabody purchased the home and remained until 1978.

It was then that Mr. Cloud Cray and Mrs. Evah Cray purchased the home. Evah wanted the home to house her extensive antique collection. The house, now a museum, includes antiques from residents of Atchison and those Evah collected throughout her life. One prized possession is a three-piece walnut bedroom set hand-carved in Germany. This item was entered into the 1893 World's Columbian Exposition and won first place for craftsmanship and beauty. In the third-floor north bedroom is a heavy handmade cradle donated by the Ronald Ramsay family. This is a particularly haunting piece, as the Ramsay family lost eight children at various times and at young ages. Some of the Hetheringtons' furniture and household items are on display in the home. A hall tree in the entryway is dated 1881 and has carved griffins on which to hang hats and coats. This item is the only piece to have always been in the home since its construction. The tower room on the third floor is decorated to honor the Crays. On the wall is a picture of the farm where they resided on the south side of Atchison. Together, they raised and raced Thoroughbred horses. Mr. Cray was once the CEO of McCormick Distilling Company, and the company's decanters are displayed in his honor. Evah Cray passed away in 1992. One of the most unusual—and potentially spirit-arousing—features of the Hetherington/Cray property is the tombstone that stands beside the house and marks the first designated town gravesite. These graves were moved when the home was being built and were then moved several more times. You can read more about this story in the last chapter of this book.

You can tour the beautiful home, now a museum, and hear about its history from knowledgeable volunteers. The carriage house has been converted into a gift shop and theater that shows a historical video about Atchison and the home.

According to oral accounts in the book by the chamber of commerce, when the carriage house was being remodeled into a theater, the new projector would not work, no matter what troubleshooting was done. The device was serviced and replaced five times. Some of Mrs. Cray's items were placed into a display case and moved into the home, and the technical issues immediately stopped. It was as if Mrs. Cray was finally satisfied that her belongings were in a safe place and on display. Another account related to the home tells of a Bible that is moved to various locations, and each time it is found, it will be opened to different passages. Many feel that Mrs. Cray is still watching over her precious collection of antiques. We took a tour while in town and Goldie, the volunteer tour guide, was very knowledgeable and told us stories of her ancestors who had worked in the Hetherington home. Come tour the house yourself, hear the amazing stories and see the precious pieces of history. But remember that your every move is being watched by someone you may not be able to see!

18

THE FARM

DANCING WITH BETSY

On any given night in the mid-1800s, residents could likely hear music playing, women laughing, bootheels thumping and men's punches landing on their enemies in the countryside of Atchison on the outskirts of town. The Farm, also sometimes referred to as the One-Mile House, as it was approximately one mile west of town, was the location for the sprawling compound that was a saloon, a brothel, a gambling venue and a dance hall owned by Betsy and John Kingston. Travelers by overland stages visited the Farm once located at 1119 Riley Street. It is reported that Artemus Ward, one of the most popular nineteenth-century American humorists, visited the Farm and declared it was the toughest place he had ever been to. Other famous visitors included the Pony Express rider Johnny Fry, Wild West criminal Jack Slade and gunslinger Wild Bill Hickock. The compound comprised approximately two acres surrounded by a high hedge fence. The lands were beautiful, with flower gardens, fruit trees and grapevines. The interior decor of the house was one of the most immaculate in the country. The carriage house held silver-mounted harnesses. Thousands of dollars changed hands each night in this luxurious location of unsavory fun. The place was not for the cowardly, as fights were an hourly occurrence. Although beautiful and lavish, the Farm was where one went to be entertained, but also struck, stabbed and killed.

John Kingston, an emigrant from England, came to Atchison with the circus but left the show due to a quarrel with his employer. John also was an expert three-card monte shark who traveled the country making his money.

Betsy was from Rushville, Missouri, and had been married previously to a man named Bryant. When she came to Atchison, she was a cook and housekeeper for a club of bachelors. She later took care of a location called "Fort Defiance" located on a hill prior to meeting and marrying John Kingston. Betsy, reportedly handsome, had a prominent nose that men used to shoot at to see how close they could come without hitting it. According to her obituary, Betsy was raised by "respectable parents," and an unmentioned "thoughtless act" changed the course of her life, from being a beautiful and well-educated woman to one of the most notorious women in America. At twenty-two years old, she left her hometown and began her life of debauchery. She once said she enjoyed being the known "mistress of more noted and wealthy men than any other woman in America." Betsy lived a life that you could only believe if it was a movie on the big screen.

Betsy met and married John Kingston in 1855, and together they built and opened the Farm. Betsy and John had a son named Tom O'Brien. Tom learned well from his parents and became a gold-brick counterfeit expert. He died in prison while serving a life sentence after killing his partner, Kid Waddell, in France.

Dances with the ladies who lived and worked at the Farm cost fifty cents, so every song played put approximately twenty dollars in Betsy's pocket. Currently, twenty dollars is equivalent to seven hundred dollars. Patrons were reportedly drugged, robbed and murdered at the brothel. According to an article in the *Atchison Daily Globe*, Dave Cook recalled a story that he once remembered having to handle when he was the provost marshal. Billy Duffield, of Company D, First Colorado, got into a dispute with a woman and her lover, Jack Cook, at the Farm. As Billy and Jack argued through the locked door, Billy threatened to kick the door in. Billy proceeded to kick down the door while Jack Cook grabbed his gun and shot Billy in the head, killing him instantly. The next day, a mob of angry residents burned the home, first allowing the girls who worked there to remove their trunks of belongings. A mob of several hundred men organized to lynch Cook, but the law protected him from that fate.

This forced the pair to move to Colorado and open the Island, a hotel, corral and barn. But trouble followed them, or maybe it was the nature of the brothel business. A soldier was accidentally shot in the saloon entrance. After the early release of his murderer, several hundred soldiers burned the Island to the ground. All that was saved were two horses. With that, Betsy and John moved back to Atchison, reopened the Farm and ran it, enjoying its greatest success, until 1886.

In November 1886, Pat McKay, a Missouri Pacific worker, was staying at the brothel. Intoxicated, he began abusing a woman who worked for Betsy. John Kingston pulled Pat off of the woman he was choking. John was mauled by Pat in the altercation. But he successfully removed Pat from the premises, grabbed his revolver and chased Pat down in his nightclothes, firing his gun into the night in Pat's direction. John injured him with a flesh wound, and both men were arrested. Dave Cook recalled that when Betsy and John returned to Atchison to reopen the Farm, he fined Betsy and her husband $20 each, and he fined each girl $10 for operating illegally. Dave and other law enforcement doubled the fine every day for four days; eventually, the fine reached $960. Between the fines and the continued trouble, they eventually had to sell their belongings and move to another location. Broke and on the run again, Betsy and John moved south during the land run of Oklahoma to Oklahoma City. They were in the saloon business there for a short time. A news article reported that John Kingston was murdered in a fight with another man over a woman, but a report a year later stated that this information could not be confirmed. Another report said that he outlived Betsy, who died in 1893, and moved back to his hometown in England. About a year before her death, Betsy went to church and became very religious. A longtime friend who came to visit Betsy at the time of her death received a deathbed confession from the infamous woman.

Fred Sutton, a longtime friend of Betsy, told to the *Atchison Daily Globe* that Betsy confided in him about a murder that occurred during one of the annual ballroom events that were the highlight of the year for most patrons. Johnny Fry, the famous Pony Express rider, was in attendance from St. Joseph and spending the night at the Farm. He set his eyes on a beautiful Irish girl, but around one o'clock in the morning, Cleveland the Outlaw dropped in as he usually did at these events. Cleveland was infamous for arriving at midnight during the ball, monopolizing the women's attention and then leaving until the next year's ball. Cleveland tried to get the attention of the girl Fry had been dancing with all night, but she made it clear that she was with Fry. When Fry (also spelled Frey) excused himself to go outside, Cleveland followed. At the time, nobody knew what happened, but Fry never returned to St. Joseph to resume his mail route. Although many wild stories of his fate were told, Betsy assured her friend Fred that she knew of Fry's actual fate. She told Fred that he was murdered and buried in the basement of the Farm's house. It is important to note that news articles and the book of oral stories written by the chamber of commerce spell Johnny Fry's name with an *e*, whereas research of the famous Pony Express rider spells his name Fry. Research on

Left: Four Pony Express riders, circa late 1800s. Standing are William Richardson (*left*) and Johnny Fry (*right*). Seated are Charlie and Gus Cliff. *Courtesy Historical Society.*

Below: The location of what was once the bustling brothel known as the Farm, 2023. *Brooke Montoya.*

historical websites claims Fry died at the hands of Confederate soldiers while delivering an important message during the war. Might there be a Fry and a Frey named Johnny who were both Pony Express Riders? My research could not discern the discrepancy. Even if Fry, or Frey, is not buried somewhere below this ground that once was a location of dancing and pleasure, enough men and women took their final breaths here to have the potential for souls to not want the party to end, even in the afterlife.

Shortly after Betsy and Johnny moved to Oklahoma City, G.W. Wells placed an ad in a newspaper that he could accommodate twenty-five patients in his private insane asylum. He had purchased the house and turned it into a location for the mentally ill. It is not known how long it remained an asylum. At some point, Ira and Joan Coleman purchased the home. Trouble began to happen in this infamous spot. The Colemans were raided by the county attorney and the Kansas Alcoholic Beverage Control Unit for having liquor on the premises without liquor stamps. In September 1954, the house caught fire and burned for nearly five hours. The house that stands on the property currently was built shortly after the fire. What was once the Farm can hardly be recognized, as the city grew around the area.

Some people report hearing music playing, specifically a fiddle, and sounds of partygoers laughing and dancing. In a location with this much history of murder, mayhem and good and bad times, it's not surprising that ghostly energy is still looking to have a good time. Maybe Betsy returned to Atchison and is doing what she does best, entertaining the men of the Wild West. This location has been a stop in past years on the city's haunted trolley tour. While investigating outside in this area, I did not hear any ghost instruments playing in the distance, but I did get a series of interesting words on my word generator. The first word to appear within thirty seconds of my arrival was *alcohol*. Then I received the words *racial, sufficient, clothes, nightmare* and *belong*. After these words came in one at a time, words stopped coming. During this time, I was also talking to any spirits that might be able to hear me, asking them about their experiences, if Betsy is still ruling the roost and if Johnny Fry is really buried in these lands nearby. I also asked if any of the girls who used to work at the Farm were here, and this is when I got the words *clothes* and *belong*. The first word made me think of the story of the trunks of clothes that were spared before the house burned down. I wonder also if the girls really had a sense of belonging, as brothel workers were often cast out by their families, were orphans or were seen as women not worthy of marrying because of being unwed mothers or products of divorce. When I got the word *nightmare*, I was specifically asking about the fire that had happened.

At another investigation with my teammates from API, Tammy Christine, blindfolded, had no idea where I had stopped the vehicle. Jill Stokes was monitoring equipment in the back as we drove and walked around various locations. Tammy Christine immediately connected with what she described as a "shrill lady" with long red nails who was talking to another lady in spirit, saying, "You don't belong here." Tammy Christine felt she was talking to someone who was competition to the woman's business. She described the shrill woman as a potential madam and very greedy. She kept saying, "It's just business." On the ghost word generator, we got the word *death*. Tammy Christine explained that the woman was charming but deadly and that her mode of killing someone was poison. She also picked up on a young female whose father was possibly killed when he came looking for his daughter. She got the name *Clarice*. Then on the word generator, we got *intent, person* and *witch*. Tammy exclaimed that she had no idea where we were but that it felt like it was a brothel. I was picking up on drinking, secrets and partying. When Tammy was through, I had her take off her blindfold to look. She opened her eyes after removing the cloth and, sounding confused, asked, "Where are we?" By all appearances, the Farm today is a small, unassuming, 1950s-built home. I confirmed what she picked up on and explained the story of Betsy and the Farm to her, which she had never heard. Listen closely when you are nearby for that faint fiddle, but beware of Betsy with the long red nails, as it is "just business."

19

WAGGENER HOUSE

DEAL WITH THE DEVIL

This famous Atchison house is hard to miss, with its rooftop griffins looking out over the city. Balie Peyton Waggener constructed the sprawling estate between 1884 and 1886. The house replaced a small, wood-frame home Waggener built in 1879, which was moved to 415 West Riley Street. A beautiful Victorian home represents the boom of wealth in early Atchison. The spacious wraparound porch was added between 1894 and 1909 and has the original mosaic tile. The first floor has an open floor plan where the two living rooms used to separate into two parlor rooms, a large kitchen with a door that was once the entryway for carriages, a half bath and a large formal dining room. Much like other beautiful homes in town, the fireplaces are works of art, boasting a total of seven throughout. The second floor includes a large, open hallway with four bedrooms. Stained glass adorns the stairwell ascending, which was a trend at the time and allows colorful light to flood both floors. The third floor includes two rooms in the back that would have housed servants and a large room that was Waggener's prized legal library. The room, specifically designed to be his library, has a large window with his favorite reading chair and desk, a skylight, and sixty electric lights arranged around the room to illuminate the space at night. Waggener had an estimated ten thousand law books, the largest privately 0wned collection in the country. Located in a room upstairs is a mysterious storage space behind a bookcase that once held a safe. The basement spans the entire bottom of the home and houses a large recreation room. Behind the home is a two-story carriage house.

Waggener House, located at 415 West Riley Street, date unknown. *Courtesy Atchison Historical Society.*

Outside of town, Waggener had a five-hundred-acre alfalfa farm called Green View Farm, and he also raised livestock. His prized animals were brought and kept in the carriage house with the horses. This house has been loved over the years by its current owner, evidenced by its immaculate landscaping and magazine-worthy upkeep.

Balie P. Waggener came to Atchison as a law student in September 1866 and found his footing in law by a chance encounter with Amelia Earhart's grandfather, the successful A.G. Otis. While riding the train home from visiting a girl, Balie met Judge Otis and, through conversation, mentioned he was studying law. Otis wanted a law student and was interested in the young man but demanded letters of recommendation. Waggener returned to Atchison, ready to get his big break. He joined Otis & Glick law firm as a student but was put to the test when his duties included sweeping out the office, splitting and carrying wood into the Glick home where he stayed, caring for Governor Glick's horse and cleaning out the barn. A lot of work, but little to do with learning the law. This opportunity proved valuable, and he was forever grateful. Upon graduating he quickly opened his own practice, partnering with Albert H. Horton, and became very successful, arguing several cases before the U.S. Supreme Court. Waggener served one term in the Kansas House of Representatives and two terms in the Kansas

The house at 415 West Riley Street owned by Mr. and Mrs. Adair, 2023. *Brooke Montoya.*

Senate. He became president of Exchange National Bank in 1892 after Wirt Hetherington, successor to his grandfather, passed away.

Born in 1847, son of W.P. Waggener, Balie was the descendant of generations of old American families. Balie Waggener married Emma L. Hetherington, daughter of William W. Hetherington, who lived in the home now known as the Evah Cray Museum. He was an involved father and grandfather, eventually practicing law with his son. Balie and his son were so close that when Balie was near death, his son's voice was the only one that roused him.

B.P. Waggener became famous around the world for his picnic birthday parties for children. His birthday was July 18, in midsummer, and he held his first picnic birthday party in honor of his granddaughter Louise Waggener. Balie loved seeing the joy it brought to local children, and each year it progressed into something more extravagant. These parties were even written about in national magazines. He extended his invitations to the children of the city and later the entire countryside. Attendees were brought in by specially chartered trains to attend the circus-like picnics with free lemonade, fireworks, carnival rides, out-of-town bands and toys. In 1911, B.P. Waggener was recognized by attendee and President William H. Taft with a silver loving cup on behalf of Atchison citizens for his generosity toward the city's children.

B.P. Waggener in front of his home on September 27, 1911, sitting next to President William Howard Taft, who came to Atchison to honor him. *Courtesy Atchison Historical Society.*

Three generations of Waggeners lived in the home. Mr. and Mrs. Will Waggener, Balie's son, built a home behind his family home at 820 North Fifth Street. After his father passed, he moved back into his childhood home with his wife and children. Like his father, he practiced law and participated in politics. In 1925, the grandson moved his family into the Waggener Mansion, also a lawyer like his father and grandfather. The last of the Waggener family to live in the home was Mrs. "Wickie" Waggener. Wickie was the second wife of Will Waggener. When Wickie passed, the home's future was uncertain. The city considered turning it into a museum or a senior living center. Ultimately, it was sold to another family, who would occupy the home for generations, as the Waggeners had. The Waggener family has a spacious plot at Mount Vernon Cemetery.

In 1952, John Adair moved from Chicago to Atchison and bought the Waggener Mansion with his wife and family. Adair was the chairman of the board at Exchange National Bank. John and his wife, Jane, had four sons, John Jr., Paul, Bruce and William. Unfortunately, in 1959, Jane was killed in an accident at forty-five years old. Jane and John were with friends on their way to a fishing trip out of state when the car driven by the women was in a head-on collision. John saw the entire scene from the car of the husbands following behind. Jane's brother Paul Haskins also died at the age of twenty while still in college.

Eventually, John remarried, and his new wife and her two children joined the family and home. They lived in the home for many years until their son Paul moved in with his wife, Marsha, and they currently reside in the home. Paul Adair is the president of Exchange National Bank, just like B.P. Waggener. In working at the Exchange National Bank, Paul has grown the bank from its original single location to now five hundred. Marsha has participated in city and community events during her thirty years living in the home, but she was very clear when telling me she has had no paranormal experiences in the home. My favorite part of talking to Marsha was hearing about the home, how they have restored some features, including those in the kitchen, but that much of the home is original and being maintained with love and care.

As the legend is told, Waggener made a pact with the devil to acquire his riches. Who knows where this legend started or how it was passed and why, but added to the details are the infamous gargoyles placed on the roof to honor the pact. Thus, the Waggener House is known as the "Gargoyle House." As interesting as legends can be, they are usually inaccurate, in this case the identification of the statues as gargoyles. The statues atop the roof are griffins, which originated in the Middle East as a symbol of protection. A griffin has the head and wings of an eagle and the body of a lion and represents strength and vigilance. According to the book of oral stories by the chamber of commerce, an owner who lived in the home after Waggener fell to his death trying to remove the "gargoyles." But this story cannot be confirmed. The story of the resident falling has gained popularity and assumed a status as factual. But research does not reveal a resident's death from falling prior to the Adairs moving in or during their time at the home. Marsha confirmed that nobody in her family has died from falling, nor does she know the source of the story. Sueanne Pool and Verle Muhrer, paranormal investigators, were invited to investigate when the Travel Channel did a segment on the home. They claimed to feel the presence of ghosts, and the spirits interacted with their paranormal equipment. This house has been featured on the city's haunted trolley tour. Maybe there once was activity in the home. Maybe there still is. Maybe Mr. Waggener knows that a new family has embraced his home and that it is in good hands and doesn't feel the need to linger any longer.

20

HALLING-FRIDELL HOUSE

THE LADY IN PALE BLUE

I n a coveted location on the bluff, on a screen-protected front porch of
a beautiful home, you can enjoy the view of the Missouri River and the
Amelia Earhart Bridge, whose lights glow beautifully at night. Just south
of the bridge is the historic home of Mr. and Mrs. D.P. Blish, located at 300
R Street (Riverview Road). The current owners are restoring the home to its
original beauty and plan to offer guests the opportunity to stay as a vacation
rental. You, too, can sit on the front porch, enjoy the view and then go inside
and chat with the ghosts.

Built in 1891, the five-bedroom, three-bathroom home occupies 3,683
square feet, according to its online listing. Mr. and Mrs. Blish came to
Atchison in 1871, built their beautiful home and lived there until their
deaths, both passing away in the home. In 1871, three brothers-in-law
founded Blish, Mize & Silliman, now called Blish-Mize. Mr. Blish was the
president and founder of the company. His brothers-in-law were Edward
Mize and Jack Silliman. Their goal was to outfit wagon trains heading West.
After a few years, they successfully distributed goods to hardware stores,
lumberyards and general stores throughout the entire Midwest. The fifth-
generation descendant is currently the CEO of Blish-Mize. Having been in
business for over 150 years, the company on its website claims it is "one of
the oldest and most successful wholesale hardware distributors of our kind in
the nation." It is interesting to note that some of the Mize family lived at the
home currently called RavenHearse Manor and had descendants who lived
in the home currently called the Sallie House at one point.

Blish House, located at 300 R Street, 2023. *Brooke Montoya.*

Inside the home's first floor is a quaint kitchen with a long, narrow hallway leading into the dining and living rooms. Near the kitchen are a narrow set of stairs that would have been used by the servants leading to their bedroom and the rest of the upstairs bedrooms. The kitchen floor has a hole where there was once a bell the owner of the home could ring to call the servants. The servant's room was spacious, with a beautiful view of the Missouri River. Down the hall from this room on the second floor are the family bedrooms—two rooms and the primary bedroom. The primary bedroom has a small crow's nest. The attic is huge and includes many windows. The basement spans the entire space of the house. The home boasts seven unique fireplaces and gorgeous stained-glass windows at the foot of the stairs and above the living-room windows.

Mr. Blish died in 1907. Since the couple did not have children, Mrs. Blsih doted on her nieces and nephews, Arthur, Herber and Chester Mize and Wheeler Barlow. It is reported that Amelia Earhart attended grade-school classes in the living room of the home during the time Mrs. Blish lived there. Mrs. Blish's sister, Catherine Silliman Barlow, fell ill, and Mrs. Blish took great care of her until she passed away in 1914. Days later, Mrs. Blish was so ill that she was unable to attend her sister's funeral. It is not known what illness the two had, but Mrs. Blish likely contracted her illness from her sister. Mrs. Blish died just a few days later. Upon her death she gifted the home to her beloved nephew Wheeler Barrow, who became vice-president of Blish, Mize & Silliman at one point. He lived in the home with his wife until he passed away in 1947, and his wife, Helene, died in 1958.

While residing at the house, Mrs. Barlow hosted dinners and events for her family and also for the women of Atchison. Guests included Mrs. Waggener, Mrs. Hetherington, Katherine and Sallie Snowden and Mrs. Mize. Joseph Wheeler Barlow and his wife, as well as Mr. and Mrs. Blish, are buried at Mount Vernon Cemetery.

In 1958, a dentist, Dr. Salvatore Anthony Scemica, bought the house and lived there until 1983, when he passed away and John Fridell and Mary Halling-Fridell purchased it. John and Mary Halling-Fridell were married on May 9, 1952, and lived in holy matrimony until her passing in 2003. They had four children. John was born in 1929 in Wichita, Kansas, and was orphaned when his father passed away in an accident at work. John's life was structured from an early age. He joined the U.S. Marines and became a highly decorated officer serving in the Korean and Vietnam Wars. His awards, pictures and military honors line the stairs going up to the spacious attic. John retired in 1983 after thirty-one years of service. After retiring, he and Mary settled in the Atchison home. Mary, being very religious, had a special place next to the front door where she read her Bible and prayed. John was extremely handy with wood and every Christmas made his children and grandchildren wooden carved ornaments. John used to visit Anne Pruett, owner of Lopez De Mexico, at the restaurant every day to have his pork chili burrito and visit with her and George Pruett, Anne's husband. Anne and George Pruett are also neighbors. When John passed away in August 2020, his children sold the house to George and Anne Pruett, who are currently remodeling it and turning it into a vacation rental.

George saw my team, API of Oklahoma, drive by the house taking pictures as we were on our way out of town. He approached us with a friendly wave and after I told him my reason for snapping pictures, he graciously invited us in for a tour. On entering, Tammy Christine, psychic medium, saw the ghost of a woman in a pale blue dress on the other side of the door. Tammy Christine explained that the woman loved what George was doing with the remodeling and was very happy. She was dressed in upscale clothing from between the late 1800s and early 1900s. My intuition tells me this is likely Mrs. Blish still looking after the home she built and spent her life in with her husband. We long to return when the home is rentable to confirm this!

George shared with us stories John had told him about incidents he experienced while living in the home. John loved working on wood in the basement, and one day he heard what he thought was Mary, his wife, entering the home. He stepped across the floor into the dining room. He called out, "Mary, is that you?" She did not answer, so he thought she did not hear him. He went back to focusing on his project, and about thirty minutes later he heard footsteps again. He called out again, "Mary?" She replied, "Yes, John?" He asked her frustratedly why she did not answer him the first time. She replied that she did not know what he was talking about, as she had just returned home. The couple had many small glass figurines they liked to collect. One day when the couple was gone, the figurines were moved from the dining-room fireplace mantel to the floor in the living room. Now that George has been remodeling, he has not experienced anything. He explains that the home feels like his grandparents' home—comfortable. He is trying to change only the things that need to be done to keep the house as original as possible.

According to stories told about the home by residents who have lived there more recently, strange noises are common, especially coming from the attic. The attic has several windows that stay latched, but when the family returns home from frequent trips, the windows are unlatched and pushed open. The family living in the home during this time reports that they like to travel so frequently that they leave suitcases out for their next trip, but on waking, the suitcases have been moved to the front door as if the ghosts are urging the family to leave again. Maybe the ghost likes the solace and quiet when the family is away. Maybe they do not wish to share their home. It has also been reported that the television is turned on and the volume turned up in the middle of the night while the family is sleeping. During these incidents, there is no sign of forced entry and nothing is taken from the house, which leads the family to believe it is Mr. and Mrs. Blish ushering the family out for their next trip so they can have rule of the home. This home has been featured in the city's haunted trolley tour in past years.

CAPTAIN FRIDELL'S JERKY RECIPE
(HANDWRITTEN RECIPE STILL HANGING IN HIS BASEMENT)

Per 1 pound of meat
Slice meat less than $^1/_4$ inch thick
$^1/_2$ teaspoon salt
$^1/_4$ teaspoon pepper

$\frac{1}{2}$ teaspoon onion powder
$\frac{1}{4}$ teaspoon garlic powder
$\frac{1}{4}$ teaspoon Worcestershire sauce
3 drops Tabasco sauce
4 teaspoons vinegar
1 teaspoon Liquid Smoke

Dissolve in just enough water to cover meat. Weigh down and refrigerate for 2–4 hours. Drain and pat dry with paper towels. Lay on oven rack and bake 150 degrees with oven door slightly ajar. When dry, store in an airtight jar or container. Will keep for one year.

21

1322 MAPLE STREET

HOUSE OF THE DEAD

Built in 1926 north of Union Street (formerly known as Division Street) is the modest wood-frame home now named House of the Dead. This home was located in an area predominately known for Atchison's African American citizens. Prior to the homes in this area being built, the land was what the city called Block 56. This land was a location where buried residents were dug up and reburied when the city grew. This transition of graves in the city's history is discussed in depth in the next chapter. Eventually, the graves were removed, but over one hundred remained buried, and houses like 1322 were built on top of the land.

The people living in this home the longest were Thomas H. Winrow and his wife, Anna. They celebrated their silver wedding anniversary in 1967 at the home. A newspaper article tells of a fire at the cellar door in 1955. Other newspaper articles report disturbances and burglaries that took place at the residence. In 1968, Thom called the police, and a man named Ross was arrested for trying to break in. Additionally, Robert Ross, likely the same person, was arrested for battery, resisting arrest, assault of a police officer, and domestic disturbance when he came to the house threatening his wife, Charlotte, who was staying with the Winrows. According to the *Atchison Daily Globe* in an article published in 1975, Thomas J. Winrow died on February 28, 1966, and at the time of his death he "held interests in lots 19, 20, 21, 22 and 23 in block 40 of North Atchison." Thus, Thom likely owned several properties in the area. A news article in 1973 stated that Thom Winrow of 1322 Maple owned a pinball machine that was damaged at the Skyway Laundry. Thomas J. is buried in Mount Vernon Cemetery.

Maple Street "House of the Dead" at 1322 Maple Street, 2022. *Brooke Montoya.*

Current owners and business partners are Steve Trumble and Mike Burke, who also own Fearcation Travel, Haunted Taxi Ghost Tours USA, The Demon House. The pair have turned the home into a paranormal location for those interested in braving their fears and investigating until the witching hour. During some remodeling to get the home ready for investigations, they recovered items in walls and under baseboards. These items included an old grape soda can, a 1940s leather shoe and a 1940s black hat. These will be preserved by the new owners. Steve and Mike have decorated the home with a nostalgic midcentury feel. The living room has a box television similar to the one Carolanne gets sucked into in the movie *Poltergeist.* Each room has a theme and offers suggestions and ideas of how investigators can interact with the room and its items to get evidence from beyond.

Steve and Mike graciously met with me and Tammy Christine to give us a tour of the house. Upon driving up to the house, we noticed the home radiated an ominous feeling. While we toured the home and heard Steve and Mike's stories of what others who have investigated have experienced, Steve had a ghost word generator connected to speakers that allowed the words to reverberate throughout the house. This added an extra element of creep factor to the experience. Not long after we arrived, the word generator loudly said, "Tammy." Tammy Christine stopped in her tracks and said, "Hello" back to the house. Upstairs are several rooms, and co-owner Steve has a family heirloom he affectionately calls "Dirty Gerdy" claiming it is also haunted. Also called Gertrud, Dirty Gerdy is a doll was initially owned by a child from Poland. After Nazi soldiers invaded Poland, the girl and her family were brought to a concentration camp and the doll was taken from her. Field Marshal Goering, a German staff member of the camp, took the doll home to his daughter. Steve's grandfather was a translator during the postwar transition and was gifted the doll along with candy, cigarettes and other goods for his work. Steve's Nan gifted him the doll in her later years of life, and weird things started happening when Steve brought Gerdy home. Upstairs had more energetic pull than the first floor. Tammy Christine described seeing a little boy, Caucasian and sickly looking with dark circles under his eyes and unhealthily thin. She felt he had been buried here at some point. This was before she was aware of the home being built on the land of Block 56. Based on his clothes, she felt he had died in the early 1900s. She also saw two women, one Caucasian and one Black. The Black woman was pleading for help and would not leave Tammy Christine alone, following her all over the house. The Caucasian woman was described as having her hair pulled up, in her mid-fifties and wandering around looking for her child. The phrase "as above, so below" came to Tammy Christine audibly. After I shared with Tammy Christine the house was built on an old cemetery, we felt the statement was connected to the buried bodies left behind that were not relocated. We are above in spirit, and also below the ground. In both ways, the people were forgotten about. Left below the ground and houses built upon them and left on the earth plane in spirit with nobody paying attention. In doing research on the home, Steve told us about the death of Charles, a boy who died while sharpening his sled. This was not confirmed in my research, but he may have been a cousin or childhood friend of the Winrow children.

The basement was also heavy with energy, but a darker, more foreboding kind. During times when the house was vacant, it is believed that trespassers came into the basement and performed occult rituals. There is evidence of this on the walls and basement floor.

Steve told us that people have been touched in the home and some begin to feel ill while investigating, even having medical emergencies and needing to leave the house earlier than planned. He feels that whatever dark energy is in the house could be dangerous, and thus Steve does not allow guests to stay overnight for their safety. If you think you are brave enough to see what exactly is haunting the Maple Street home, you can book an investigation on the Haunted Taxi website.

22

CEMETERIES OF ATCHISON

UNPEACEFUL REST

In Flander's Field, O let me sleep, and wake me not and never weep for me, I rest in perfect peace." Henry Folk Lowenstein wrote this poem, noted in the *Atchison Daily Globe* when referring to the removal of bodies from one site to another. The imagery of the poem is one of eternal peace in the dead's final resting spot, but this would not be possible for many early Atchison residents. There are many reasons for the town being so haunted, but the unrestful experiences of the dead may be one of the most compelling reasons. Settling in the area for a new life or passing through for greater riches, pioneers were exposed to, and spread, diseases such as Spanish flu, cholera, smallpox and tuberculosis. The diseases spread through population groups, cities and families, often taking its victims to early graves. Some families lost multiple members to diseases with no cure. All of these circumstances make for a hard existence of grief, loss, untimely death and unrest.

During the Victorian era, many death rituals were honored and followed. People often died in their homes rather than medical centers and hospitals. Additionally, before funeral homes, or affordability, many people held the wakes and funerals of loved ones in the family home. When a loved one died, the family stopped all the clocks in the home at the time of death and closed the window curtains. The outside windows and doors were often covered with black cloth. The family wore black clothing, and friends wore black armbands, sometimes for months, to signify that they were in mourning. Some widows wore clothing of black for up to two years. The loved one's body was cleaned and dressed in the finest clothing and placed in the coffin or on a plank for viewing in the parlor. The front door was left ajar, and visitors came to pay their respects without knocking. Since catching disease was a common concern in this era, coffins were never left open for viewing once in the church or at the graveside.

Before Atchison was declared a town, the Kansa tribe had settled the riverside, along with several other tribes displaced from expansions of settlers moving West. The Kansa tribe's burial ritual involved many intricate details and was led by tribal women. They would paint the face of the deceased, wrap the body in buffalo skin and give the spirit of the deceased directions to the "land of the dead." They often buried the individual with items such as pipes, food and weapons and placed them on a hill in a shallow grave. The earliest documented grave was found in Atchison near the old Division Street Public School at North Second Street and Division Street (now Union Street) when construction began in the area. This is just north of the Sallie House location and near the likely settlement of the first Native tribes, which would be the elevated land near the Soldier's Orphan's Home and St. Benedict's College. As construction crews dug, they unearthed Native American bones with spears and arrowheads. Shortly after this, Mormon settlers were overtaken by smallpox and other diseases after setting in Atchison in the 1840s. Bones of the Mormon dead were found by workmen digging out cellars for homes or while making streets in the town. Another source notes that Mormons buried diseased dead near their settlement in West Atchison off Military Street and that the dead were decimated by the cultivation of soil over time. It is not known what happened to the unearthed bones of Native Americans and Mormon settlers. The treatment of the dead, constant movement of bodies to various burial plots, complete disregard of others and of those who were forced away or left behind, is one theory as to why spirits remain to haunt Atchison today, still in unrest.

EVAH CRAY MUSEUM GRAVE MARKER

The first graveyard established and used by citizens was on Fifth Street where W. Hetherington's house was later built and today is known as the Evah Cray Museum. A marker still stands in the yard of the home to signify the spot of Atchison's first cemetery. Established in 1856, this location was

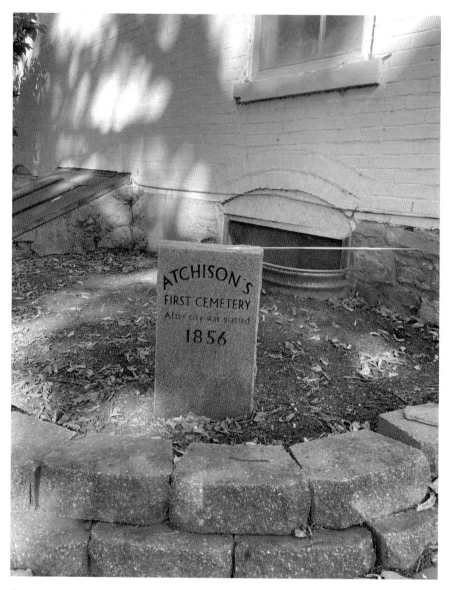

Grave marker outside Hetherington House, which held the first established graveyard in the city before expansion and more homes eventually being built there, 2022. *Brooke Montoya.*

quite a distance from town, but after experiencing the boom of westward expansion, the community needed space to build homes for its growing numbers of residents. Their solution was to uproot the dead and move them.

BLOCK 56

General John H. Stringfellow reserved "Block 56" on the hill in far northwest Atchison, again farther away from town. For a long time, this was the cemetery for citizens, taking in those previously laid to rest near Hetherington's home on Fifth Street. As the city boomed quickly with more residents, Block 56 was no longer suitable; more homes were needed. Eventually, Oak Hill Cemetery was established in the 1860s. The bodies of those buried in Block 56 were moved and buried at Oak Hill. For some of these bodies, it was the third time they had been relocated. Unfortunately, families had to pay for this, and not all of them could afford it. Furthermore, some of the deceased no longer had living relatives to arrange for their move to Oak Hill. Thus, over one hundred bodies were left behind at Block 56. Headstones were removed, the land at Block 56 was fenced and eventually what lay underneath was no longer identifiable by looking at the land. John Matthews, a local citizen, plowed up the soil and grew a vegetable crop on the land. As time passed, houses were built on the lot, and the bodies were never recovered. One house with paranormal activity on the lot of Block 56 is the Maple Street house discussed in Chapter 21. In this area, people have reported seeing apparitions and hearing voices of the dead and forgotten. John Price, who established the Oak Hill Cemetery, once said, "So soon are we forgotten when we are dead." At one time, this location was part of the city's haunted trolley tour.

OAK HILL CEMETERY

Oak Hill is situated one mile west of the river and is elevated, overlooking the city. The final resting place for many of the moved bodies that went unclaimed was Oak Hill Cemetery. The cemetery was established in 1865, and the trustees included prominent citizens like James Martin, George W. Howe and J.M. Price. A number of early settlers were initially buried at Oak Hill Cemetery, but many residents reburied their loved ones in Mount Vernon Cemetery after it opened. The remains were buried next to one another in rows regardless of sex or color. In the southwest part of the cemetery, Grand Army of the Republic (GAR), the fraternal organization for Union veterans of the American Civil War, have graves marked by a white wooden cross. A large cannon guards the graves of the veterans. Before I knew that bodies had been relocated to this cemetery, we drove through out of curiosity and an appreciation for cemeteries. Of course, cemeteries are burial places for the dead and are overall sad, but this cemetery had an even greater sadness as if the heavy grief of being forgotten hung like a thick smog over the land. On the west side of the cemetery is an entire section of children's graves dated anywhere from the 1930s to the late 1950s. It is not known who these children are and why they are not buried with family.

An interesting grave in this cemetery is of J.C. and R.D. Reisner's children. Etched onto a tall white stone reaching into the sky reads, "Children of J.C. & R.D. Reisner," and the stone proceeds to list two children on each side of the monument. Beside the monument are small gravestones with each of the eight children's names. Gertrude, Burton, Ella, William, Anna E., Rebecca, Martha and Mary were children of J.C. and R.D. Reisner, and they passed incredibly young, many before the age of two, but all deaths were on different dates. While taking pictures and deciphering the names on the worn gravestone, we got the words *building*, *rental* and *destruction* on the ghost app generator. Researching the Reisners, I located a hotel property J.C. owned as a leasing property. It also appears that Reisner Park, located at 619 North Tenth Street, was named after this prominent Atchison family that experienced so much loss. Unfortunately not much else can be located through my research about the Reisners and what happened to their family. Haunted stories of this location are passed among the city's residents. One account is that one night, the police were called to the cemetery with the belief that kids were in the cemetery past closing time. The police investigated, but no one had been in the cemetery. No one alive, that is. The caller had actually seen a ghostly apparition.

MOUNT VERNON CEMETERY

This cemetery is where many of the well-known citizens of Atchison reside in death. It was dubbed the most notable and beautiful in Kansas during its early construction. Incorporated in 1864, adjoining the city of Atchison, it is located at 6920 Rawlins Road. The initial sales of graves exceeded anticipation when the cemetery opened, selling for between five and ten dollars per lot. The cemetery overlooks a beautiful lake, with some graves nestled near the edge as if to enjoy the view of the water for eternity. Residents here include squatters, governors, senators, heroes, railroad engineers, hoaxers, pioneers and a citizen featured in "Ripley's Believe it or Not!" The first burial was the infant son of Louisa R. Gerber on May 5, 1864. The next twelve buried were also children. In its earliest days, Mount Vernon was segregated, with African American citizens buried to the left of the entrance road. This was not an uncommon practice of the time. A section of the cemetery on the north end is referred to as the "Pauper's Field." It is a section of unmarked graves. Those with unmarked graves in an earlier time were people who could not afford to purchase a plot, criminals or those who took their own life. An interesting monument is that of "Little Ned" Rigg. He died at the age of seven in 1887. His monument was carved using a picture of him and measurements provided by his parents. The carved beauty represents him frozen in time, writing a letter to his mom on a scroll.

Among the notable pioneers and settlers of Atchison buried in this cemetery are Atchison's earliest resident, George M. Million; Samuel Truehart, a former enslaved man who came to Atchison from the exodus; the richest man in America, Luther C. Challiss, whose land was purchased to build the cemetery; and "Kansas' Most Fascinating Person," William "Deafy" Bouler. As of 2021, there are approximately fifteen thousand graves. The first tombstones were made from the native limestone or sandstone. On the UHaunted Taxi Tour, the guides Mike and Steve ask guests if they want to "touch a ghost." On entering the cemetery, there is a grave to the left of the path of a person the guides call Mr. Young. Steve with UHaunted uses his SLS to help you know when your hand is close to the ghost. There is a section the guides call "whisper alley." Walking through this area, you can hear faint ghostly whispers. Near the first pine tree in the cemetery, many have reported seeing an apparition standing. An old legend established is if you look at the Dye tombstone, you soon will die. There is no truth to this, but seems to be a lore told among the youth to add the spooky feel of the cemetery. Although at night the cemetery may include sightings of ghostly guests and whispers, during the day, the cemetery is a sight to behold.

MOUNT CALVARY CEMETERY

The Catholic cemetery, formerly known as St. Benedict's Cemetery, is located at 9950 Highway 7 and was established in 1863. Mount Calvary is the final resting place of many Irish immigrant residents, like John McInteer and Michael and Kate Finney. This cemetery is smaller than Oak Hill and Mount Vernon. In this cemetery, toward the far fence line, are two side-by-side rows of children's graves. According to the Benedictine Parish, this area is referred to as "Baby Land" and is a location for families to bury their infants at a greatly reduced price for those in financial need.

KANSAS CHILDREN'S HOME CEMETERY

This cemetery is the final resting place for children of the orphanage. It is on the property that used to be the Soldier's Orphan's Home, established to nurture, educate and maintain indigent children fourteen and younger of soldiers and sailors who served in the Civil War. When the war ended, the location was owned by the state and included abandoned and neglected children who had become wards of the state. The property is now private and owned by Benedict College, located on the northeast part of town near the water tower. Some buildings of the orphanage are still standing. In 1907, Edgar Beckwith, a child who lived at the orphanage, drowned while bathing in Deer Creek. In 1907, Edgar's grave was dug and covered with a homemade blanket, and the children of the home laid flowers over where he lay. For unknown reasons, he was not buried where the other four bodies at that time were buried and the initial Orphan's Home Cemetery was established, because in the newspaper the day after Edgar's death it was reported that the four bodies were "taken up" and moved approximately a quarter of a mile to be buried near Edgar. Billy Kingsley, a nine-year-old boy, was laid to rest in this cemetery after he died in the hospital of an infected appendix. The cemetery is approximately one hundred square feet, and many of the graves are unmarked.

BIBLIOGRAPHY

Books

Adams, K. *Atchison Kansas: Portal to Other Worlds*. Atchison, KS: self-published, 2013.

Atchison Area Chamber of Commerce. *Haunted Atchison: The Collected Stories*. Edited by Justin Pregnot. Newton, KS: Mennonite Press, 2011.

Dickson, Gary D. *Atchison, Kansas: Memories of Years Past*. Atchison, KS: Atchison Daily Globe.

Haegelin, F.M. *The History of the Haegelin-Ziebold Family*. Atchison, KS: self-published, 1981. Available in Atchison Historical Society resources.

Ingalls, S. *History of Atchison County Kansas*. Lawrence, KS: Standard Publishing Company, 1916. Project Gutenberg's History of Atchison County Kansas. http://www.gutenberg.org.

Mize, W.R. Various unpublished writings.

Park, Richard A., II. "The Party: No Party Was Ever Held Like This Party." Unpublished manuscript. No date.

Pickman, D.L. *The Sallie House Haunting: A True Story*. Woodbury, MN: Llewellyn Publications, 2010.

Pregont, J., ed. *Haunted Atchison: The Collected Stories*. Newton, KS: Mennonite Press, 2011.

Sachs, D., and G. Ehrlich. *Guide to Kansas Architecture*. Lawrence: University Press of Kansas, 1996.

Tonsing, E.F. *Heroes, Hoaxers, and Haunters: The Symbols, Stones, and People of Mount Vernon Cemetery*. Atchison, KS: self-published, 2021.

Waggener Family, Hetherington Family, and Munich Family. (n.d.). Atchison Historical Society Collection.

Warner, C. *Theatres.* Atchison Historical Society Collection, B–1183; 2021.0832.

Woods, R.B. "The First Frontier: Kansas and the Great Exodus." Chap. 3 in *A Black Odyssey: John Lewis Waller and the Promise of American Life.* Lawrence: University Press of Kansas, 2021.

Newspaper Articles

Atchison Church Visitor. "Happy Hallow." August 5, 1916.

Atchison Daily Champion. November 24, 1885; April 13, 1909.

———. "Baby Played with Matches." December 26, 1902.

———. "'Betsy Kingston': One of the Most Notorious Characters in America Is Dead." October 28, 1893.

———. "Bodies Moved." July 2, 1907.

———. "Carl S. Otis Dead." May 24, 1910.

———. "Death of Mrs. John Dye." January 25, 1911.

———. "Funeral of W.W. Hetherington." February 2, 1892.

———. "Gerrish Baby Dead." December 22, 1915.

———. "A Home Child's Funeral: Burial of Little Edgar Beckwith." July 1, 1907.

———. "An Interesting Tree: Story of a Lynching Bee in Atchison in 1863." January 26, 1893.

———. "John Kingston." August 17, 1881.

———. "Mrs. D.P. Blish Ill." February 3, 1914.

———. "Park's Party: It Is Stopped but a Few Guests Evade the Officers." May 16, 1901.

Atchison Daily Free Press. "The Mount Vernon Cemetery." May 10, 1865.

Atchison Daily Globe, July 16, 1894; March 8, 1900; March 6, 1915; June 27, 1921; October 13, 1921; June 22, 1973.

———. "A.C. Trueblood Died." April 16, 1904.

———. "Barlow Rites." January 7, 1958.

———. "Catherine Silliman Barlow Dies." February 5, 1914.

———. "C.C. Finney Died." March 29, 1947.

———. "City News." May 12, 1921.

———. "Dr. and Mrs. S.A. Scimeca 22 June 1973." January 5, 1964.

———. "Encephalitis Fatal to Richard Stanton." June 19, 1966.

———. "E.O. Bradley, a Suicide." March 1, 1913.

———. "The Farm." May 2, 1881.

———. "Fine Harness Horses Once Raced on Taylor Track in Atchison." December 31, 1961.

———. "Governor Glick Is Dead." April 13, 1911.

———. "The Island." September 11, 1897.

———. "Ilva True Attending School." June 2, 1913.

———. "Ilva True Visiting the Finneys." July 31, 1913.

———. "Judge A.G. Otis Dead." May 7, 1912.

———. "J.W. Barlow Died, 69." July 15, 1957.

———. "Kingston." October 3, 1890.

———. "Kingston." February 22, 1899.

———. "Kingston." August 7, 1902.

———. "Laura C. True Files for Divorce." May 6, 1904.

———. "Local Woman Killed, Another Critically Injured in a Car Accident." October 11, 1959.

———. "Magazine Publishes Hat Picture." October 19, 1899.

———. "Miss Ella Earhart." December 3, 1907.

———. "Miss Trueblood Services." October 22, 1959.

———. "Mistaken Identity." October 2, 1891.

———. "Morrow Came to Town." April 5, 1854.

———. "Mrs. A.C. Trueblood Died." January 19, 1924.

———. "Mrs. Speed Stanton Dies." October 31, 1973.

———. "Mr. Waggener." April 29, 1918.

———. "National Fashion Show." September 20, 1899.

———. "Oak Hill Cemetery." June 20, 1921.

———. "One Life Lost: Copeland Hotel, at Topeka, Destroyed by Fire." January 14, 1909.

———. "Pat McKay." November 24, 1886.

———. "Perry Johnson, Fired from Job, Hung Self." April 9, 1895.

———. "Property Destroyed." December 15, 1887.

———. "Tom O'Brien." December 30, 1904.

———. "William True Has Stroke." November 13, 1916.

Atchison Daily Patriot, January 26, 1880; September 22, 1888.

Atchison Weekly Globe. "Barlow Hosts Party Guests." August 25, 1921.

———. "Billy Kingsley." May 20, 1926.

———. "C.C. Finney." October 16, 1905.

———. "Day's Doings." July 21, 1910.

———. "Finney Gun." January 27, 1910.

———. "George G. Orr Drowned." July 29, 1909.

———. "George Littleton." May 25, 1903.

———. "Mr. and Mrs. William True Marry." May 15, 1913.

———. "Mrs. D.P. Blish Donates Altar." April 27, 1911.

———. "Mrs. G.W. Glick Passes Away." September 18, 1919.

———. "Mrs. Waters." April 16, 1925.

———. "New Building for Mt. St. Scholastica's." September 2, 1915.

———. "William A. True and Agnes Marry." May 8, 1913.

———. "William A. True, Engineer True Passes Away." May 9, 1918.

———. "Zibold and Finney Marry." November 10, 1904.

Kansas Zeitung (Leavenworth, KS). "Kingston." September 11, 1858.

May, Joey. "City of Atchison to Recognize History of Racial Violence." *Atchison Globe*, May 27, 2021.

Myers, M. "Atchison Post Office Provided Reflection of Town History." *Atchison Globe*, July 2, 2015.

Websites

Andreas, A.T. "William G. Cutler's History of the State of Kansas: Atchison County Schools." Roots Web. 1883. www.sites.rootsweb.com

Arensberg Pruett Funeral Home. "John Fridell of Atchison, Kansas, 1929–2020, Obituary." 2020. https://www.arensbergpruett.com.

Baniewicz, L. "Atchison Street with Racial Undertones Is Changed from Division to Unity Street." *The Leaven*, July 31, 2020. www.theleaven.org.

Benedictine College. "Benedictine Professor's Research Leads to Confirmation of 1870 Lynching in Atchison." www.benedictine.edu.

Boise City Ghost Hunters. "Paranormal Research and Investigations Society." 2009. https://boiseghost.org.

———. "A Trick of the Mind or the Supernatural? Unexplained Phenomena at the Glick Orr House." www.boiseghost.org.

Centers for Disease Control and Prevention. "1918 Pandemic." www.cdc.gov.

Clarisa. "Unhappy Ghost." Only in Your State. September 2017. www.onlyinyourstate.com.

Elite Paranormal of Kansas City. www.spectre.eliteparanormalkc.com.

Haunted Taxi Ghost Tours. www.hauntedtaxi.com.

Historical Marker Project. "Lincoln School." Accessed 2023. https://historicalmarkerproject.com.

History.com. "Spanish Flu." www.history.com.

Howey, J. "Atchison Remembers the Tragedy of George Johnson." *Atchison Globe*, June 11, 2021.

Kansas Historical Society. "George W. Glick." www.kshs.org.

National Archives. "The Deadly Virus: The Influenza Epidemic of 1918." www.archives.gov.

National Park Service. "Exodusters." www.nps.gov.

National Register of Historic Places. "Kansas (KS), Atchison County." www.nationalregisterofhistoricplaces.com.

Pickman, D.L. "The Sallie House." www.salliehouse.com (no longer active).

Velvet Ropes. "Sallie House: The History of this Atchison Kansas Haunted House." www.velvetropes.com.

Weiser-Alexander, K. "Haunted Atchison: Most Ghostly Town in Kansas." Legends of America. August 2021. https://www.legendsofamerica.com.

Podcasts

Criminology Podcast. Larry Sarvey.

Videos

City of Atchison. "Footprints 29." YouTube, June 16, 2017. www.youtube.com.

KMBC 9. "Ghost Stories: Atchison Railroad Legend." YouTube, October 31, 2008. www.youtube.com.

McIntosh, Nathan. "Sightings: Heartland Ghost Sallie House Haunting." YouTube, June 18, 2018. www.youtube.com.

ABOUT THE AUTHOR

Brooke Montoya is a Licensed Professional Counselor, a Licensed Alcohol and Drug Counselor and a Certified Hypnotherapist. She owns a private practice in Oklahoma City that approaches healing through holistic alternative wellness and counseling. She has taught full-time at the University of Central Oklahoma and as an adjunct at Southern Nazarene University for over nine years. She is currently completing her dissertation toward a PhD in human development and family science at Oklahoma State University. As a sensitive, she reads tarot cards and is a Certified Reiki Master. Brooke is the founder of Afterlife Paranormal Investigations of Oklahoma and has over eight years' experience as an investigator. Her team travels nationally, investigating locations and researching the afterlife. She is also a member and investigator for the Warren Legacy Foundation for Paranormal Researchers, started by Chris McKinnell, grandson of Ed and Lorraine Warren. This is her first published book, but she has published an award-winning curriculum on co-parenting, community fact sheets and workbooks. She also has three boys and two dogs that are the loves of her life. Author website: https://bmontoyaauthor.wixsite.com/Montoya. Afterlife Paranormal Investigations of Oklahoma website: https://apiofoklahoma.com.

FREE eBOOK OFFER

Scan the QR code below, enter your e-mail address and get our original Haunted America compilation eBook delivered straight to your inbox for free.

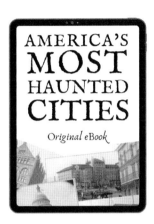

ABOUT THE BOOK

Every city, town, parish, community and school has their own paranormal history. Whether they are spirits caught in the Bardo, ancestors checking on their descendants, restless souls sending a message or simply spectral troublemakers, ghosts have been part of the human tradition from the beginning of time.

In this book, we feature a collection of stories from five of America's most haunted cities: Baltimore, Chicago, Galveston, New Orleans and Washington, D.C.

SCAN TO GET
AMERICA'S MOST HAUNTED CITIES

Having trouble scanning? Go to:
biz.arcadiapublishing.com/americas-most-haunted-cities

Visit us at
www.historypress.com